BLACK

What Black Folks
Should *Really* Know
About Financial Planning!!!

& GREEN

a book by

RICK KNIGHT

Atlanta, GA

Copyright © 2005 by Rick Knight
Second Printing: 2006

ISBN: 0-9759870-0-3
Library of Congress Card Number: 2004096730

Rick Knight
www.BlackandGreen.net

Printed in the United States

DEDICATION

For my Father who taught me the
value of a dollar

For my Mother who gave me one every
now and then

"Whether I am the hero of my life or whether
that station shall be held by another,
these pages must show."

--Charles Dickens
From the book, David Copperfield

Message from the Author:

First, thank you for taking the time to read this material. Whether you purchased this book, received it from a friend or if you are standing in the aisle of Barnes & Noble thumbing through the pages, I thank you. I do not promise that all the information will leap from the page at you like those of a mystery novel, but I will promise you that when the words on the following pages collide with your gray matter, there will be an information explosion. Few African-American Financial Advisors endeavor to put this type of information together, but the popularity of the lottery in black culture proves that we want to be wealthy, that we want to live a comfortable life in our retirement and after reading this book, I feel confident that you can realize those dreams.

Consider this book your lottery ticket with much better odds. I have read over twenty books and a litany of magazine articles addressing financial planning, but none of them address core socioeconomic issues that are exclusive to Black Americans. Let's be real, Black Americans and white Americans are different and society treats them accordingly. Financial planning and investment strategies historically have not been dinner table conversation in most black homes. I agree with Toni Morrison who is credited for saying "If there is a book that you want to read, and it hasn't been written, you must write it." So here we are.

With all due respect to my fellow black authors, enough books on making us feel good about ourselves have been written. I have never been more passionate about anything in my life, with the exception of trying to be a good father. I believe that if we Blacks had a blueprint on how to invest effectively, it would force us to become more active in investing and take a more proactive role in becoming educated in investment strategies. It would also force Black America to become more politically aware as to who is truly looking out for our best interests. It would empower Black America on a global level, whereby we would not be recognized solely as the largest group of consumers in the United States. It would get our children involved earlier and remap our thinking of the new American dream.

Whether due to fear of the unknown or the fear of losing our hard earned money or just not having access to certain information, African-Americans have consistently missed the wealth boat in building wealth through investments such as stocks, bonds, mutual funds or even taking advantage of company sponsored profit sharing plans such as the 401k. Well, together we can change that.

Give me two weeks of your life and you will be more equipped to make financial decisions that will benefit you and your family. It is time for us to become gold medallists in the game of investments and retirement planning and I am confident that these pages will arm you with the information to accomplish that. You will be challenged and at times it will not be easy, but if you absorb the information on these pages you can achieve your investment and retirement goals. This is your tap on the shoulder and we are in this together. Tomorrow will not be a more opportune time. Right here and right now is the time for you to go forever forward!

Enough of that. Let us get to work!!!

In all toil there is profit, but mere talk tends only to want

>Proverbs 14:23

TABLE of CONTENTS

PREFACE

From the very outset of this book, I am going to ask for your undivided attention. It is my sincere belief that this is one of the most important books you will ever read with respect to your hard earned dollar. It's purpose is simply to change your life. From the selling of the first African slave, blacks have been involved in the commerce of this great land we call home. Black people have had to become self sufficient and endured circumstances that were be unimaginable. Blacks have had to rely on themselves from learning how to read (with the fear of a beating hanging over their head like dirty laundry) to counting, saving, and investing. For those of you who reading this book, you will never know of those conditions. But just for a second, try to place yourself there. There has to come a time when as Black Americans we own the responsibility for creating and retaining our own wealth, own the responsibility of speaking a new language, and own the responsibility of creating legacies for generations to come. I believe that the time is now. This book's intent is not to allow you to jump on the 'I am black and downtrodden wagon', but rather the 'educate and empower' wagon.

I believe that it is important to start this journey as far back as history allows us. It will provide invaluable insight on how the powerful black dollar reached from there to here. There has been a psychological dislocation of Black America that has impacted most facets of life, especially the ability to generate a substantial income over an extended period of time and to save and invest monies.

Records show that the first group of Africans to set foot on what is the United States of America were brought to South Carolina but later fled to live with the Indians. The census of 1851 identified 3,498,057 Africans in the United States. Of these, 11% were free and the remaining 89% were enslaved. This is where I would like to begin. In my opinion it is here that Africans (we were not African-Americans then), began to take shape of a financial foundation that exists today.

In 1877, the Liberian Exodus Joint Stock Company had been formed in Charleston, South Carolina. This company purchased a ship, the Azar and by May of 1879, plans were being made by southern blacks to migrate north for a better life. The Azar subsequently was highjacked and sold. When suit was brought against the perpetrators by the Liberian Exodus Joint Stock Company, it was not entertained as a valid claim.

Rugged individualism has been the companion to Black Americans for hundreds of years. The resistance to allow Africans to enter the workplace as equals was inevitable and in 1866 white workers met and formed The

National Labor Union. It was this union's purpose to represent all working people. However, African-Americans were never accepted as equals and thereby never received proper representation, based on the claim that African-Americans did not fully understand the true principles of labor unions. Blacks were not admitted as full members. So in 1869 African-Americans came together and formed the National Negro Labor Union with the express purpose of advancing the cause of black workers.

Now let me stop right there for a moment. This book is not intended to point out the indiscretions of whites versus blacks. We all know of the injustices and unfairness that have taken place over the years and some of our black leaders have made careers reminding us of those injustices. The purpose here is to discuss solutions and take a proactive role in understanding the destiny of your future. My theory is this:

While all of these injustices were going on, former slaves collected enough money among themselves to capitalize a business that turned out to be of no value when the money disappeared from the white-owned bank. These types of practices punished black businesses for years and most black businesses failed. For years the inability of African-Americans to control the economics of their own community meant the failure of the attempt for social reconstruction. I will not horrify you with the stories of inhumane treatment suffered at the hand of frightened white oppressors. As I stated earlier, that is not the purpose of this book.

At one point in history Thomas Jefferson was given the task of drafting a declaration calling for the separation from Great Britain. It was the following clause that some historians and scholars argue that because of its omission is adequate proof that Africans were never meant to share in the fruits of independence and equality. This clause was omitted at the request of delegates from the southern states of South Carolina and Georgia and some northern delegates who benefited from the slave trade. This is what was left out of that important document:

"He King George III has waged cruel war against human nature itself, violating its most sacred rights of life, liberty in the persons of a distant people who never offended him. Capturing them and carrying them into slavery in another hemisphere or to incur miserable death in their transportation thither. This piratical warfare these infidel powers is the warfare of the Christian King of Great Britain, Determined to keep open a market where men should be bought and sold he has prostituted his negative for surprising every legislative attempt to prohibit or restrain this execrable commerce."

Had these words been printed it would have been the president, Thomas Jefferson himself denouncing something that was going in his own back yard.

Through the years Black America grew up, both socially and economically. As far back as 1810, the first black-owned insurance company was established. It's original purpose to provide Black Americans with a proper burial. By 1841 society had seen its first black millionaire in the person of Mr. William A. Liedesdorff who was born abroad and sailed to California to find his fortune. In 1888, the country's first two black banks, the Savings Bank of Grand Fountain United Order of True Reformers in Virginia and the Capital Savings Bank in Washington, were established.

Throughout history there have been a litany of factors that have stunted the growth of African-American prosperity, such as the peonage system which allowed blacks to be arrested for the smallest infractions (or in some cases nothing at all) and then forced to work for white businesses and landowners for no pay. On the heels of the peonage system, were the "Black Codes". These so-called codes imposed heavy penalties for vagrancy, insulting gestures, curfew violations and seditious speeches. South Carolina went so far as to require a thousand dollar bond from blacks entering the state and agree to give their white employers the right to beat them. Before that, in 1793, the state of Virginia passed a law forbidding free blacks to enter the state at all.

But through all of that, the African-American spirit has survived and thrived.

Frederick Douglass wrote "the only thing that America owes you is the opportunity to succeed." That is the essence of these writings if we do not remember the past we are destined to repeat it. But that was then and this is now.

The Black population numbered 35.1 million or 13% of the total population in 1999, with a majority still in the south. In 1999, 33% of the black population was under the age of 18 compared to 24% of whites (non-Hispanic). For the population 65 years and over, the figures were 8% and 14% respectively. There were 8.4 million black families and 53.1 million white families in 1999. One of the most telling and disturbing statistics is outlined below and I really want you to digest these numbers:

47% of all black families were married-couple families, 45% were headed by women with no spouse present and 8% were maintained by black men with no spouse. In stark contrast, white families were 82% married, 13% headed by women with no spouse and 5% men with no spouse.

We as black people should be ashamed of those statistics. Taking into consideration the unforeseen human factor, such as death, there isn't any real statistical difference in the proportion of black married couples and of those headed by single black women.

I know these simple truths may be difficult to swallow, but as my dad use to say, "figures don't lie, liars figure." Black America continues to lag behind in every major category. For example: The percentage of Black Americans 25 years of age and over with a high school diploma or higher degree is 11% lower than whites. When it comes to post secondary formal education of at least a bachelor's degree, it is even worse with a thirteen percentage point difference. Further, a higher percentage of black women earn college degrees (16%) than black men (14%). Again I echo, we should be concerned by these figures.

These statistics are not only troubling but they have a detrimental domino effect when it comes to the labor force and quality of life. This book's mission is to hopefully help level the playing field. In March 1999, there were 16 million blacks and 102 million whites, 16 years and older, in the civilian work force. Blacks made up 12% of the civilian work force compared with 74% of whites. The proportion of employed white men, 32%, in managerial and professional specialty occupations almost doubled that of black men. In 1998, 52% of all white families and only 28% of all black families had incomes of $50,000 or more, and poverty levels are consistent with these numbers as well.

If Black Americans do not begin to embrace individualism and responsibility for self and family, I fear that these statistics will get worse. The ideology that you are "owed" something or you have an automatic "entitlement" by virtue of your skin color (even if it is true) is outdated and that belief system should be dismantled immediately.

I spread my dreams under your feet, tread softly friend, for you tread on my dreams - Yeats

CHAPTER ONE

WHY DOESN'T BLACK AMERICA INVEST?

Without knowledge and vision, a people will perish.

The title of this chapter is less of a question and more of an outcry. Why Black America will not invest could be an entire book within that one question. However, I will concentrate more on the solutions and ways to motivate you to act, instead of echoing what we already know.

During a conversation with a friend of she told me the story "Grandmother and the Shoebox." She said when she was growing up she noticed that her grandmother always had cash in a shoe box or in a handkerchief knotted and pinned to her bra. (It brought back the memory of my own grandmother reaching into her bra for cash before sending me to the store).

As I grew older I asked my grandmother why she didn't keep her money in the bank. Her response was this: "When I was coming up, blacks weren't allowed to do business at the banks and when we did, often times the banks weren't fair to us and blacks' money often disappeared," so she didn't trust the bank.

Now that the banks appear to embrace black businesses, we as blacks have now been conditioned to think that the bank is the only safe place to put your money for savings and investing. That is the furthest thing from the truth! As now is the time to dismantle that storefront mentality. Ask yourself this; do you think that the titans of wealth or those that have accumulated a large amount of assets stand in the local bank lines?

After passing all of the tests to acquire my securities license and undergoing all of the FBI background checks, I remarked to a friend of mine, *"the system* has messed up and let me in the club."* I figured that the knowledge I was equipped with would have Black America flocking to me as bees to honey, but that was the furthest thing from the truth. Black Americans became my worst source of clients and I often found that the information and knowledge that I had to share was flatly rejected and that caused me to wonder, why? What the hell was going on?

Mr. John Rogers, founder and CEO of Chicago based company, Ariel Capital Management, is said to have made it his mission to "get African-Americans talking about Wall Street and Wall Street talking about African-Americans." One of the most amazing discoveries Mr. Rogers has made in his surveys over the last twenty years is that African-Americans are 35% less likely to invest than their white counterparts. Furthermore, he found that the majority of blacks make real estate and life insurance their primary investment vehicles.

I surveyed one hundred African-Americans from all walks of life, from a drug dealer to a minister and everyone in between asking the question, "why don't blacks invest?" Individuals from the lowest end of the economic ladder to some of the wealthiest individuals I could find participated and surprisingly, some of the responses were the same.

DELAYED GRATIFICATION vs. INSTANT GRATIFICATION

We live in a world of instant everything. Microwave this...we want everything NOW! NOW! NOW! If you listen to advertisement on so-called black radio, it encourages getting that pre-owned Lexus, NOW! Buying that big screen television, NOW! Need an extra $200 until payday? Come get it, NOW!

The most startling discovery I made when asking why we responded to this type of advertisement was that we as blacks would rather *show off what we have.* We want to be seen and make a statement of material gain as opposed to saving and investing in our future and the future of our children. We want to live for the here and now versus securing our future. We want to consume things instead of investing in those very things that we consume. Ask yourself, do you know someone who has an expensive car, and yet lives in an apartment? Or someone who has the most expensive of everything but is probably two paychecks from being put on the streets or may be drowning in debt? Maybe that someone I'm describing is you.

I reject that thought process and I

encourage you to dismantle that belief system. If you are going to be a consumer, become a better consumer. Instead of buying a pair of $200 Nikes, for example, buy a share of solid stock. Or, purchase stock in Sony instead of purchasing a Lincoln Navigator. True, no one will be able to see those purchases you've made, but in the long run you will realize the long-term benefits of those purchases. The car and those shoes are going to get old and lose value and you may have to throw away or trade them. Good stock purchases from good companies will be around forever.

Below are the top ten responses I received from my survey asking why blacks don't invest. See if one of these would be yours.

1. I don't have money to invest
2. I am living paycheck to pay check as it is
3. I don't know
4. Fear
5. Nigga get outta my face
6. I have some other things going on right now; when I tie them up, I will be ready
7. I have something at the job
8. My husband takes care of that
9. I am not thinking about the future right now
10. I don't understand that investment stuff

I would like to address number 10 first because it's the response I may be able to help you the most with. Furthermore, I think if you have a better understanding of something you will be able to make better use of it; like having all of the ingredients to a recipe.

This entire book is dedicated to helping you understand investment and retirement planning better. There is an old saying "ignorance is bliss," and as long as people don't know something, they don't have to take responsibility for acting on it. (That is the same excuse people use for not wanting to go to the doctor.) "As long as I don't know I have it, I don't have it." When it comes to our financial future, we must divorce ourselves from that thought pattern.

Many black Americans have been conditioned to believe that the United States Government will take care of them in their old age. This is not the case, and really never has been. It's now time for personal accountability. My parents were born in the 1930s. They grew up working and taking care of children, with the promise of social security and pensions if they stayed at a company for thirty years. And that's exactly what happened. There is honor in that, and they taught their children the same values. However, times have changed dramatically. There was no 401k plans for the majority of their working years, no Internet, no tech stocks, stock options or computer and technology industry.

Black Americans have access to the accumulation of more wealth than ever before, yet the wealth accumulation gap of white Americans vs. black Americans continues to widen. Black Americans are the largest group of consumers in America. It's high time to also became at least one of the largest groups of investors.

For those of you who gave the same response as number 9, I say this, "THINK ABOUT IT!!!" The biggest concern that older Americans and those getting close to retirement have is out living their income. Simply ask yourself, "if I don't take care of my future, who will?"

For those of you who leave it to your husbands, response number 8, please pay close attention to Chapter Five *For Da Ladies*.

For those who have "something at the job", number 7, there has been a proliferation of fraud, thievery and outright lying in Corporate America that has left many Americans without any retirement. The likes of Enron, Global Crossing, Adelphia, WorldCom and Consolidated Freight name a few. Americans, both black and white, who have given years of their life ended up with very little or nothing. It is my firm belief that everyone with a company pension should privatize a portion of his or her retirement. That way you'll have total control no matter what happens to that job. Find a good financial advisor, one that has your goals and objectives as his or her priority, and let it be someone you can trust.

For the number 6 responses, there will never be a perfect time. Even if you have to start small, just start. I've heard this advice for so long, I don't even remember who said it, but it holds true. "Pay yourself first" and stop waiting.

For those of you who are brave enough to say number 5, I offer you this. One of my dearest friends shared his father's advice: "If you hang out with nine broke niggas you are bound to be the tenth one". Enough said.

Number 4, fear, is a common response. However, I believe that knowledge will neutralize fear. If you know what the hell you're talking about, you will have confidence to make the decisions that are needed. That is what I am confident this book will do for you. The media would much rather report bad news than good. The talking heads and political pundits seem to get a tingly feeling all over when they have the power to scare you.

However, when you have information of those things they do not report on the nightly news then you can invest with confidence. It is time to get off of the sidelines and get in the game.

1, 2, and 3 are somewhat tied together, and money seems to always be the number one excuse. I want you to ask yourself, "do I have a $750 Lincoln Navigator or Cadillac Escalade monthly car payment?" How many big screen televisions and designer shoes I have? I'm not saying this to be condescending, but I do challenge you to take a look at those things.

Remember, Black Americans are the largest group of consumers and people usually purchase what they want, not necessarily what they need.

Consider yourself the CEO of your own company, and every dollar that you have is an employee. Now, you can fire those employees, by spending them and I promise you, they will have no problem finding work elsewhere and growing someone else's company. Or you can keep them, and let them continue to work for you to let your company grow.

It will not happen overnight in most cases. But, if you are diligent and committed you can change your future. Let's talk about the vehicles that we will need to get us there.

CHAPTER TWO

INSURANCE

*How much sweeter the fruit of my father's labor
would have been if he had tasted the knowledge
of these writings*

I used to hear my grandmother and even my parents say, "child all I need is enough insurance to bury me with." However, accumulated wealth and expanding your net worth, "just enough to bury you with", will not be enough to cover taxes and provide for the loved ones you leave behind.

With all of our concerns in today's society, purchasing life insurance seems to slide further and further down the list of priorities. But ask yourself this, "If I were to die right this second what would happen?" I know your heart would stop beating, but what would really happen? If you have a spouse and kids, if you are an only child and are taking care of a parent, if you have a home, what would happen? When the last sprinkle of dirt is out of the shovel and the last mourner has left your gravesite, will you have left your loved ones better off, worse off or the same as when you were alive? Because African-Americans invest a large amount of money on insurance, we are going to spend some time in this chapter.

Most people - not just African-Americans spend a lifetime running from insurance agents, but a good agent can be a very valued asset. Before purchasing an insurance policy, ask yourself the following questions:

- How much insurance do I need?
- How long will I need insurance?
- How much income do I provide for my family? Does anyone depend on my income (parents, children, spouse, grandparents, siblings)?
- Do I have children for whom I'd like to set aside money to finish their education in the event of my death?
- How will my family pay final expenses and repay debts after my death?
- Will there be estate taxes to pay after death?
- How will inflation affect future needs?
- What is the right kind of life insurance for me?
- Do I have insurance on my job?

After answering these questions, you are well on your way to securing a life insurance policy that will fit your specific needs and those of your family.

Complete the following *Life Insurance Needs Analysis* to help you determine what amount of life insurance coverage you may need.

INSURANCE NEEDS ANALYSIS
How Much Insurance Do I Really Need?

List all known Assets

Cash & Savings $_____
Investments $_____
Real Estate $_____
Current Life Insurance $_____
Pensions $_____
Social Security (if any) $_____

List All Debt (present & future)

Mortgage $_____
College Savings $_____
Daily Living Expenses $_____
Daycare $_____
Automobiles $_____
Outstanding Loans (revolving & installment)
$_____

Immediate Expenses

Attorney Fees/Probate $_____
Outstanding Medical Bills $_____
Annual Salary of deceased $_____
Funeral Cost $_____
All Additional Debt $_____

Line #1 Total of all assets $_____

Line #2 Total of all debt and immediate expenses
$_____

Line #1 subtracted from Line# 2

equals

Immediate insurance need $_____

I have found one of the most common responses to why black Americans will not purchase life insurance is:

I am young and single, why do I need life insurance?

The answer to that question is a simple one. Mother Nature is going to play the same cruel trick on you as she has played on all of us: you are going to get older. You may get married, have children and purchase a home; and as your estate or financial posture improve, so does your responsibility. You must address future tragedy in the present. Not only is life insurance very cheap for you to buy at a young age, but you are probably in the best health of your life.

Here is another reason. Suppose you are diagnosed with a condition such as diabetes, cancer or some other disease that would make you uninsurable. It will be too late to purchase life insurance at that time. Just like a car, it's better to have one and not need it than to need it and not have it. As a rule of thumb the head of household should have seven times his or her annual salary in life insurance. This may not seem like a lot. The important thing is to at least start working toward this goal.

Also keep in mind that practically every policy your employer provides you with is temporary coverage and more often than not terminates when you leave your job. You should always privatize a portion of your life insurance where you alone control it.

With all of the stubbed toes in life, we face various amounts of risk such as disability, sickness, accident, unemployment, and premature death. It is the premature death that plays the biggest part of your life insurance needs.

There are very few vehicles that will allow you to give them $25 dollars a month and if you meet a premature death will pay your named beneficiary $50,000 $100,000 or maybe even $150, 000.

Over the years, life insurance has grown up and become as sexy as we have ever seen it, and life insurance is being used as an investment tool now more than ever. There are several types of life insurance. These policies can be used separately or in combination with one another depending on the individuals needs. Recent

31

figures from the life insurance industry breakdown life policy purchases as roughly 24% term life, 55% whole life and 21% universal and variable universal life policies.

We are going to vigorously discuss various insurance products in this chapter to provide you with the knowledge to make the right choices for you and your family. From the time I sold my first insurance policy until now, I have felt that there has to be a better understanding of what the consumer is buying. I sat with a middle-aged woman once who had been sold a policy and had no earthly idea what she had purchased. The goal of this chapter is to answer the questions about various types of life insurance products. So put this book down and go get your policy and let's go over it together. If you do not have a policy, please keep reading. This will be sort of a hands-on crash course. When it comes to purchasing life insurance there is no "one size fits all." What may be a good policy for one person or one family may not meet the same needs for another individual or family. You have to decide what purpose you want your insurance to serve.

There are really only two categories of life insurance: **permanent** and **temporary.** They are broken down further into six major types. We will cover the permanent vs. temporary coverage debate with a very detailed chart. On the following pages all combinations are derived from these six basics: **Term Life,**

Whole life, Adjustable life, Universal life, Variable life and Variable universal life. So let us begin, shall we.

Term Insurance

What the heck is that?

Term Life is temporary insurance that provides protection for a specific term of years only. It may be issued in *renewable, convertible or no-renewable policies.* Basically, you are renting your insurance and unless you have a crystal ball and know the exact moment you will drop dead, this type of coverage is not the best to purchase. The term may be for one, five, ten, or twenty years and up to a specific age, or anything in between. The policy has NO cash value and will pay benefits only if the insured dies during the specified term. If the insured dies after the term, you get NOTHING.

If you have a $250,000 term life insurance policy it is almost the equivalency of having a $250,000 dollar lottery ticket. The insurance company is not giving you this policy because they are nice people they want to make a profit and in most cases you will outlive that policy and get nothing. (*Hint:* If you have insurance with your employer, it is probably this type).

There are three types of term policies:

Level Term

Level term will provide a level death benefit and level premium during the policy term. For example: If you purchase a 10 year-term policy with a face benefit amount of $100,000 dollars, it will remain in force for ten years provided you continue to make the premium payments for ten years. Should you die, your named beneficiary would be $100,000 wealthier.

Decreasing Term

Decreasing term is a temporary policy as well. The face amount of the policy decreases throughout the life of the policy down to zero at the date of policy expiration. This type of insurance is appropriate for individuals having a declining need for coverage over time (like mortgage protection insurance).

Decreasing term is usually issued as *convertible* but generally is not renewable at the end of the term period. The convertible feature allows you to convert to permanent insurance at some point while the policy is in force.

Adjustable Premium Term

Adjustable premium term in my opinion, is the worse insurance policy on the market and let me tell why this "appears" attractive. It starts with a very low monthly premium and gradually increases every year. As you get older, your premium becomes more and more expensive. Bear in mind you have no cash value built into this policy and these policies usually will expire at age eighty. Let's say James is 40 years old and purchases one of these policies. In 40 years at age 80, the policy expires. He has just paid an insurance company 40 years of his hard earned money (see chart) and has nothing to show for it. He has no insurance and because of his age he cannot get any insurance coverage. So always inspect your insurance policy.

As with all things, there are advantages and disadvantages – sort of like marriage - but I digress.

Advantages of Term Insurance

- Initially, the cost of term insurance is low and accordingly it is often used by individuals or businesses that may have a large need for insurance but limited financial resources to pay for it.

- As temporary protection, it is often used to help cover temporary needs.

- Term insurance can be flexible. It is frequently used to provide additional protection for an insured. For example, a husband has a relatively small whole life policy and becomes a new daddy of triplets. His responsibilities have suddenly changed. Term insurance could be a quick and inexpensive way to address this issue.

And now the bad news:

Disadvantages of Term Insurance

- The very nature of term insurance is a disadvantage. It is temporary protection for a limited period of time. If the policy is not renewable or unaffordable due to the increasing cost of the policy, the insured can be left without insurance at a time when he or she needs it most (old age) Some experts put it this way, term policies are designed to expire before you do.

- Over a long period of time, term insurance becomes very expensive, even more expensive than whole life policies. A 20-year policy bought at age 35 would have a significantly lower premium than the same policy bought at age 55.

- Even though the premium for decreasing term remains level for the term of the contract it pays less and less insurance. In the later years of decreasing term policy, the actual cost of the remaining insurance tends to be expensive.

- Term insurance is pure death protection only. It offers no living benefits such as guaranteed cash values.

- Even if the term policy is renewable, it generally is not renewable beyond a certain age, such as 65 or 70.

Although Term insurance can fulfill certain protection needs over a certain period of time, it is not a pure investment vehicle simply because it does not have the potential to provide any type of cash value build-up. If you don't die you don't get anything.

Whole Life Insurance

The first policy of life insurance on record was issued in 1563. All policies issued for the next 200 years were either short-term or endowment. The few whole life policies that were written had no determined face amount. In 1762 the whole life, level premium policy was born. This is what we know today as "whole life" or "permanent" insurance.

Whole Life insurance offers insurance coverage for – you guessed it - your whole life. If you are insured under this type of policy it will pay you the face benefit amount one day, one year, ten years or 75 years later after you purchased it.

The premiums for whole life policies are level and guaranteed for the life of the policy. There will not be an increase in the premium amount. Simply put, The premium WILL NEVER CHANGE.

Not only does the premium remain level for the life of the policy, but so will the face amount of the policy. It may even increase and that will put you in a much better position.

Another feature of a whole life policy is its ability to provide a guaranteed living benefit at the policy's cash value. Usually, during the first few years of the policy, the cash value (living benefit) will be zero, as you have not had time to build a cash value. But it will increase steadily up to age one hundred. The cash value is exactly the amount of the face death benefit. (By the way, your insurance company will consider you dead at age 100 so try to hang in there. You are entitled to the face amount of the policy.)

With Whole Life policies come many options as to how it should be designed to best serve you. These come in the form of **riders.**

ALERT!!! As you may be aware, for many years Black Americans have been charged more for the same amount of coverage than our white counterparts in these types of policies.

What you have to be aware of in a whole life policy is keeping track of your cash value. Often a dishonest agent or company will take your cash value and apply it to a policy that has no cash value without your knowledge, or take the cash value that you have accumulated in one policy and purchase new products while telling you that the policy will cost you nothing. Well, guess what? It just cost you your entire cash value of one policy and you have to start all over again building cash value in the new policy.

Further, a less than honorable insurance company will take cash value in a whole life policy and repurchase term insurance for the same face amount should the whole life policy lapse. This leaves you, the policy holder, thinking you have no coverage even though often there is some type of coverage still in force (this happens mainly with the elderly). When the policyholder dies, the beneficiaries make no claim believing that there was no coverage when in fact there may have been. So review those old policies!

For example:

Emma purchased a whole life policy with a $50,000 dollar face amount. After having this policy for ten years, Emma built up a cash value amount of $10,000. Emma suddenly became ill and couldn't make her monthly premiums any longer. The insurance company may take that money and purchase term insurance (remember, it's cheaper) for $50,000 face amount for as many years as the $10,000 cash value will buy. Emma may believe that she has no insurance and then later dies and her beneficiaries will think the same thing when in fact some slick insurance company may owe Emma's estate $50,000.

My suggestion is to go back through all of those old policies, find the whole life policies, and for those that were never redeemed, call the insurance company to find out its status. You may be surprised at what you find. Become the designated family insurance policy checker. Check the policies of your mom, dad, etc.

The cash value may also be borrowed, but you do not have to pay back the loan unless you want to. Show me a bank that will let you do that. Bear in mind, if you choose not to repay the loan, it will reduce the face amount by the amount that you borrowed. For example; Fred has a whole life policy with a face amount of $50,000. He borrows $10,000 worth of cash value from the policy and chooses not to repay it. At the time of Fred's death, his beneficiaries would receive a death benefit of $40,000. $50,000-$10,000 = $40,000.

There are four main types of whole life policies:

Continuous Premium Whole Life - This is the most common type of whole life insurance sold. These policies stretch the premium payments over the whole life of the insured (to age 100). This policy is also referred to as straight life.

Single Premium Whole Life - is simply a whole life policy with one premium payment. The entire cost of the policy is paid in a lump sum instead of paying over your lifetime. What this will accomplish is a discount of premiums and it has all of the same characteristics of continuous whole life.

Limited Payment Whole Life - These policies allow you to pay for the entire policy in a short period of time; ten, fifteen or twenty years. The premiums for any whole life policy can be broken down into any desired number of installments. Because more premium is being paid, the policy's cash value will be higher than continuous pay whole life.

Economatic - is a whole life policy with a term rider that uses dividends to purchase additional paid up insurance. Let's assume that you wanted $100,000 dollars of whole life but couldn't quite afford it. Instead, you purchase $80,000 of whole life and $20,000 of term insurance. Thus, you have your $100,000 of death protection at a lower cost and when the paid up additions equal $20,000; the insured now owns $100,000 of whole life but only pays an economical premium for $80,000.

There are also many different riders that can be placed on your whole life policy.

Advantages Of Whole Life Insurance

- The primary advantage of whole life insurance is that it is permanent insurance, not temporary like term policies. It can be used to satisfy permanent needs such as cost of death, funeral and final burial and it offers peace of mind.

- The level premium allows you to always know exactly the cost of insurance and allows you to plan for it better.

- Whole life builds a living benefit through its guaranteed cash value benefit which can be used for emergencies, purchasing a home and ultimately as another stream of retirement income.

Disadvantages of Whole Life Insurance

- The premium-paying period may last longer than the insured's income producing years

- The policy does not provide as much protection per dollar as a term policy

Depending on the needs of your family, there are many ways to design a plan. Ask a lot of questions and get the plan that fits your circumstance best. We have discussed the traditional types of life insurance; permanent and temporary (whole life and term).

There are a number of life insurance policies that have been designed to fit specialized needs and they have taken on quite a few different forms. We will discuss three of them.

In recent history, several new types of life insurance were born, which can give you more flexibility with your investment dollar. They are adjustable life, universal life, variable life and variable universal life respectively.

Let's start with Adjustable Life, shall we?

Adjustable Life Insurance - This policy offers you the option to adjust the policy's face amount, premium and length of protection without ever having to complete a new application and barely blinking an eye. This plan gives you the flexibility to convert to any form of coverage because it is based on the money purchase concept. The basic premise is not so much as to which policy you buy, but how much you spend on premium.

For example: If you have $600 a year to spend on premiums you should take into account your circumstances and situation and what the money would provide you and your family most. This policy can grow and change with you as you and your family grow and change.

Universal Life - This was the insurance industry's answer to the extremely high interest rates we experienced in the decade of the seventies. In an effort to become more competitive, many insurers developed this product with relatively high interest rates. These policies provide a high level of flexibility. You (the policy holder) may:

- Increase or decrease the death benefit
- Change the premium amount as long as enough premium is paid to maintain the policy.

BE CAREFUL! This type of policy does not have a specified death benefit and it can fluctuate depending on the interest rate and consistency of premium payments. In essence, you have a one-year renewable term life, with a cash value benefit as well.

Most universal policies are sold based on the accumulation values and tax deferred retirement income rather than on a proposed death benefit. For example: Let's assume you have a universal life policy with a premium of $500 annually for $50,000 of coverage. When the premium is paid, an amount necessary to provide one-year renewable term coverage is used to cover the death protection element of the policy. The balance is deposited into a cash account where it will earn competitive current interest rates.

BE CAREFUL! There are actually two interest rates associated with the universal policy (the current year guaranteed rate and the contract rate). The current rate can change every year (this is the one the agent will concentrate most of his energy on). The contract rate is the minimum guaranteed interest rate, which the policy guarantees, would be paid, (this rate is usually a considerable amount lower than the current rate). *If you are not one to take any risk when it comes to your life insurance, this is not the policy for you and neither are the next two*

Variable Life - Although a relatively new concept in the United States, variable life insurance has been marketed in Europe for many years and it is said to have been marketed in the Netherlands in the mid 1950's. Many consumers have become more investment oriented and wanted the luxury of a life insurance policy with some investment options. Variable life insurance offers the potential of greater benefits and higher cash values than whole life insurance.

Variable life insurance provides a death benefit that varies according to the investment performance of one or more separate investment accounts maintained by the issuing insurance company. The benefits payable from the insurance contract and the contract's cash value will vary with the investment experience of the separate account. The separate account(s) that are established to fund the variable life contracts may be invested according to a predetermined investment objective in common stocks, bonds, money market instruments or other investment vehicles. It is called the separate account to distinguish it from the insurance company's general account, because those funds are used for fixed benefits and separate accounts benefits are not a fixed amount.

BE CAREFUL! The amount paid as a death benefit varies according to the success of the investments in the separate account.

These plans usually have a guaranteed death benefit that may increase over the life of the policy. Cash values are not guaranteed and often are determined daily.

It has been said this type of insurance is a whole life policy designed to protect the policy owner and the beneficiaries from the erosion of their life insurance dollars due to inflation.

Therefore, it could be said that variable life is designed to be a hedge against inflation.

FAIR WARNING! It's my belief that this type of policy is well suited for today's younger investor who does not have a great deal of family liability. Although there is risk involved, with methodical planning and commitment, the good out weighs the bad.

ALERT! -Because this is considered an equity product, an agent will need more than just a life insurance license, he must have a series 6 or 7 and a 63 securities license because these types of contracts are regulated by the Securities Act of 1933. Make sure your agent is properly licensed.

FYI - At the time of the solicitation, variable life illustrations may not be based on projected interest rates greater than 12%. This prevents the agent form assuming excessive and unrealistic rates of return and is know as the *12% rule.*

Variable Universal Life – This is a combination of variable life insurance and universal life insurance. The benefits of this plan are that they combine the best features of both plans. The policy is variable in that the benefits vary according to the investments backing the contract. Also, many companies will allow you to choose the type of investments you favor. This is the kind of company you want to do business with. You decide which investments you believe will provide for the greatest return on your hard earned dollars.

FYI - This type of policy is not best suited for the "laid back" investor. If you like to be in the thick of things, this is the policy for you.
    The policy is universal in that it has a flexible premium, adjustable benefit, term or endowment insurance and a tax deferred savings. The flexible premium allows you to choose the amount of your premium payment. The adjustable feature allows the insured to change

the benefit. The premium payment will then become the amount needed to provide such benefit. Both the premium payment amout and the benefit amount are dependent on the performance of the stock portfolio backing the contract. The term and endowment features provide life insurance protection at a low cost and retirement income respectively.

That's it. Those are the insurance vehicles that will be included in your retirement portfolio, one way or another. If you have dependents and limited cash on hand, one of these products will best suit you in your quest for creating an estate.

There are many other types of insurance such as health insurance, auto insurance, disability insurance and long-term care insurance. Though some are needed, they do not give you the chance to generate or create wealth.

Chapter Summary

With all families comes major responsibility as well as a truckload of everyday decisions when designing a life insurance plan. Just remember that there are six basic types and however you design your plan, it will include one or all of them.

In today's economy the need for insurance is substantial. Because of its diversity in the industry insurance can serve as both an investment/savings vehicle as well as a nest egg and asset protection for your loved ones when you kick the bucket. Or in its most modest form, it can simply provide you with a proper burial. Whatever way you decide to use it, it is still going to be your best bet dollar for dollar. Sit down by yourself or with a loved one and evaluate which types of coverage will be most suitable for you and then act. I would strongly urge that you use all the resources that you have at your disposal (i.e. the Internet, library, and speaking to more than one insurance agent or broker). If you are new to the insurance market speak to a friend who knows or can recommend someone to you.

Notes

CHAPTER THREE

INVESTMENT VEHICLES
*It is through the eyes of knowledge that we
see more clearly.*

Once I was speaking with a 28 year-old hair salon owner who said to me, "Rick, for one year I decided to write down and keep track of every penny I made for the entire year." She said that by the end of the year she had earned over seventy thousand dollars. She told me that at the end of that one year period the only money she had to her name was the money she had made that day and she didn't even have a car. She decided right then and there that she needed to do something else with her money, but she didn't know what or how.

My dad worked in construction for thirty-seven years. Every time he built something, he needed a blueprint and the proper tools to get the job done. Now that you have gone out and earned your money, we will endeavor in this chapter to get a clear understanding of the investment tools that are available to help you "build your retirement home". Before we decide on an investment strategy, we must first understand how each investment works and how it can work for you.

The greatest challenge I see facing African-Americans in beginning their investment life, is getting educated and actually getting started. We must first learn to think differently about investing and planning for retirement. We must learn the language and talk the talk of investing. My dad once told me that, "in the absence of a roadmap, any path will take you there." Now before you say anything, I'm pretty sure he didn't make that up, but he was the first one I heard say it. Consider this your roadmap. It's my firm belief that the more you know the more comfortable and motivated you will be to start investing.

One of the biggest myths for years was, "you need a whole lot of money to make money in investments. Well that is simply not true any longer. Mutual funds have become a very popular vehicle. Mutual Funds are the chameleon of investment tools; they can serve the multi-millionaire as well as the college student, the single mom as well as the young couple that just starting to build a nest egg.

Statistically, 88% of American adults own a mutual fund. If you were to really look at that number, you would find that black American adults that own a mutual fund are still almost non-existent in the big picture, but at least we have joined in, no matter how small the percentages. 68% are above the age of forty, 60% have incomes of between $30,000 and $100,000 and a very high percentage have less than $1,200 in the bank. If this describes you, nothing to feel bad about, you are in the majority.

There are a litany of investment tools you can use to reach your financial objectives, but the eight most commonly used in today's investment community are:

1. Annuities
2. Mutual Funds
3. IRAs
4. Employee Provided Pension Plans (401k)
5. Stocks
6. Bonds
7. Certificates of Deposits (CD'S)
8. I-Bonds

Since the mutual fund has become the most popular and diverse investment tool of late, we will address it first.

What is a mutual fund?

A mutual fund is a company that brings together money from many people and invests it in stocks, bonds, or other securities. Its combined holdings are known as the *portfolio.* Each investor owns shares, which represent a part of these holdings. Mutual funds allow people with the same common financial goals to pool their money together. There are more mutual funds to invest in than there are stocks on the New York Stock Exchange.

Mutual funds can be a good way to invest in stocks, bonds, and other securities. The mutual fund has become the duct tape of American investments. It offers the following benefits:

- Mutual funds are managed_by pro-fessional money managers
- Mutual funds allow you to diversify your holdings so that all of your eggs are not in one basket. This allows you to spread out your risk and create an environment for a much better return.
- Mutual funds buy and sell large amounts of securities at a time. The costs are often lower than what you pay on your own. It's sort of like Wal-Mart or Home Depot. They go out and make bulk purchases and then sell to you at a cheaper price.

Mutual funds allow you to invest any sum of money. With certain minimum requirements, they can be pledged as collateral for a bank loan and they have an automatic reinvesting provision that will ease your tax burden a little.

You can always find out the value of your shares on the financial pages of major newspapers after the fund's name. We will learn how to read the financial page later. Bear in mind, all mutual funds have a certain amount of risk involved. It's up to you and your advisor to determine how much risk you want to expose yourself to. The bigger the risk, the bigger the potential reward.

As an investor, you can purchase mutual funds in many ways. Like IRA's, the banks want you to think that they are the only place on earth where you can purchase a mutual fund. Well they aren't. You have many options and remember, you are in charge. It's your money.

Although most funds are sold through brokers, financial planners or insurance agents, you can purchase some funds by contacting the company directly and with the assistance of the Internet your options are limitless. I will warn you though. If you are not an experienced investor, I strongly urge you to speak with a professional or you could very easily find yourself on a ledge in the middle of the night wondering where you went wrong.

There are many types of funds and they earn you money in three ways:

- First, the fund may receive income in the form of dividends and interest on the securities it owns. A fund will pay its shareholders nearly all of the income it has earned in the form of dividends.

- Second, the price of the securities a fund owns may increase. When a fund sells a security that has increased in price, the fund has a capital gain. Usually, at the end of the year, most funds distribute these gains, minus any capital losses to the investors.

- Third, if a fund does not sell but instead holds on to the securities that have increased in price, the value of its shares increases. This pushes the value of your shares up and if you sell you will earn a profit.

Before choosing a fund, it's important to know what funds are out there and how they can help you reach your goals. We are going to look at nine major types of funds. This will give you a very good mixture of how to best design your own portfolio.

1. Growth Funds

These funds consist largely of common stock and seek growth of capital through appreciation in the market of their investment. They typically invest in stocks of companies with the greatest potential for long-term growth These could include companies in fast growing industries, such as technology or healthcare.

2. Value Fund

In contrast to a growth fund, a value fund focuses more on companies that are temporarily out of favor with the market so their stock may be selling for less than their estimated worth. These stocks are usually with well established companies that investors have overlooked or companies experiencing a positive change.

Growth vs. Value

Historically, growth and value investments tend to react differently during the economic cycle. Since value stocks are often more driven by cycles in nature, they may benefit from the increased spending that usually occurs during an economic expansion. Growth stocks on the other hand may also perform well during an expansion, but they usually prosper during a slowdown of the overall economy. So when building a portfolio they both play an important part.

3. Income Funds

A fund that has high current income and a high rate of return, primary objective seeks to earn interest and dividends almost exclusively. Most income funds invest in high yielding bonds and preferred stock in an attempt to maximize current income.

4. Specialized Funds

A specialized fund does exactly what it says; it specializes in a specific industry or geographical area such as the health care industry or tech stocks or the entertainment industry. Its policy is to invest at least 25% of its assets in a particular investment sector.

5. Balanced Fund

The balanced fund is the gray suit of growth funds. It's the most conservative and its objective is to achieve both growth and income with a conservative investment approach.

6. <u>Bond and Preferred Stock Funds</u>

Bonds and preferred stock funds are for the investor with very little tolerance for risk. It places it emphasis on the safety of principal and income earned through interest and dividends.

7. <u>Municipal Bond Funds</u>

Municipal bond funds seek current income by investing exclusively in municipal bonds. These funds are attractive because of the tax-exempt interest passed on to shareholders from investing in general obligation bonds and revenue bonds.

8. <u>Government Bond Fund</u>

Government bond funds are considered the most secure fund in terms of capital preservation. These funds invest in only U.S. government securities of different maturities.

9. <u>Money Market Funds</u>

Money market funds consist of liquid assets with short term maturities of usually less than one year. The objective of this fund is to provide current income, high liquidity, and although they are a great place to temporarily park funds during an uncertain period such as job change they are not good for someone seeking long term growth.

One last thing about money market funds; there is a big difference between a money market account at the bank and a money market fund at the bank. Some less than honorable banks are remiss in making this distinction to keep your money in their institution. Just remember:

- A money market fund is a type of mutual fund. It is not guaranteed and comes with a prospectus.
- A money market deposit account is a bank deposit. It is guaranteed and comes with a Truth in Savings form.

As we know, there is a certain amount of risk involved with all mutual funds. There are also certain tax consequences. You will owe taxes on any distributions and dividends in the year that you receive them. You will also owe taxes on any capital gains you receive when you sell your shares so keep your account statements in order. If you invest in a tax exempt fund, such as a municipal bond fund, some or all of your dividends will be exempt from federal and sometimes state and local tax. However you will still owe taxes on any capital gains. We have used that word, capital gains, often in this chapter without really addressing exactly what capital gains and capital gains taxes really are. It's very quick and dirty: A capital gain is a realized gain from the sale of securities.

Aside from taxes, there are some ongoing

expenses related to a mutual fund:

SHARE CLASSES

As an individual investor, when purchasing mutual funds there are four main share classes that will affect you as an individual investor; A shares, B shares, C shares and No Load funds. You will have to pay a sales load or sales charge when a mutual fund is purchased. It usually pays for commissions to people who sell the fund shares as well as other marketing costs. If you are new to the world of investments, whether you have a sales load or not, is very important. If you have a sales load you also have professional broker services and advice and although that will not assure a greater return, it definitely will help guide you through the investment maze. The three main share classes that you will be exposed to as an individual investor are:

A Shares - Also known as a Front End Load, is a sales charge you pay when shares are purchased. Under the law, this type of load cannot be more than 8.5% of your investment. When you are investing long-term, this share may serve you best.

For example: If you have $1,000 to invest in a mutual fund with a 6% front end load, $60 will go to pay the sales charge and $940 will be invested.

B Shares - Also known as a Back End Load fund, does the opposite of its brethren; the Front

End Load. This sales charge is what you pay when you sell your shares. It usually starts out at 5 or 6% for the first year and gets smaller each year after that until it reaches zero. You must be careful with B shares. As your investment grows you could end up with higher 12b-1 management fees.

C Shares - This fund has little or no front end load, but often charge higher annual fees that will increase as the value of the fund grows

No Load Funds - These funds have no sales charge and have become very popular, but be careful. Companies that market these funds are not doing it because it gives them a warm fuzzy feeling. They offer no professional assistance in choosing funds or any professional advice and they generally have higher 12b-1 fees.

ADDITIONAL EXPENSES

It is important to review all materials once you begin investing. There are ongoing expenses that you will be charged and it is nice to know where every penny of every dollar you invest is going. Always look at the fee table of your statements. This table will tell you the management fee along with any other fees and expenses.

Note: High expenses do not assure superior performance.

Rule 12b -1 fee - It most often pays commission to brokers and other sales persons, and occasionally pays for advertising and other costs of promoting the fund to investors. It is usually between 0.25% and 1.00% of assets annually. Note: Funds with back end loads usually have higher 12b-1 fees.

Take that into consideration when purchasing your shares and if you really like to read, review the fund's annual and semi-annual reports. If you request one from the fund they will send it to you.

ANNUITIES

Annuities are probably the most misunderstood and under utilized investment vehicles on the market. Hell, it's even hard to spell. If it's confusing to you, then you are not alone. One of the major reasons for the confusion is that there are so many variations of annuities. Although there are three basic types, many people don't know what they are and how they perform. But, they've been around for a very long time.
What is an Annuity?
An annuity is a financial contract made between you, the owner, and a life insurance company. In return for payment of one or more deposits, depending on your choice of annuity, the insurance company agrees to provide you either a regular stream of income or a lump sum amount in the future, usually at retirement or age

fifty nine and a half. If you are wondering why this age is chosen, that is when you may begin taking distributions without incurring any penalties.

As I mentioned earlier, Annuities come in three flavors:

1. Fixed
2. Equity Index
3. Variable

FIXED ANNUITY - Offers you the safety of your principal and a rate of return for a set period of time guaranteed by the insurance company. When the guarantee period is over, the insurance company offers a new rate for the next determined period.

Food for thought - The fixed annuity is a wonderful investment vehicle to add to your portfolio if you have a very low risk tolerance. It will lock in a guaranteed interest rate and if the economy does better than your rate of return you could miss out on some upside growth. For example: You purchase an annuity with a guaranteed rate of 6% and someone invents something better than Viagra and the average rate of return is 10%. Well, by you locking in at 6% you will miss the other 4% growth. However if there is a downturn in the market - to say 4% - you will come out ahead.

Equity Index - This is a special type of fixed annuity in which earnings credited to the contract are based on a formula connected to an independent stock market index such as Standard and Poor's 500 Stock Index (S&P 500)

Variable - This annuity will offer you a selection of investment portfolios within the annuity that will fluctuate in value over time and could be worth more or less upon **annuitization.**

How does it work?
You deposit money with the insurance company. In turn, those deposits are invested by the insurance company in to one or more securities portfolios and earn income or capital appreciation tax deferred until paid out to the annuitant. Annuities have two phases:

Phase #1 - This phase is referred to as the accumulation phase; it begins as soon as you invest your deposits. Your deposits purchase accumulation units in the insurance companies separate account. These **separate accounts** invest in securities portfolios which are created and administered solely for the benefit of the annuity and you begin accruing what is called accumulation units. Each one of these units represents a proportionate share of the net assets of the portfolio. In other words, it's like an upside down whole life insurance policy. Whereas a life insurance policy will pay your beneficiaries when you die, an annuity will pay you a guaranteed sum and certain income as long as you live. Should you choose that option, studies have shown that people with annuities tend to live longer. Although there are many different options when choosing an annuity, there are really only two ways to purchase an annuity, Single and Flexible Payment. Depending on your situation, you can choose the one that best suits you. Of course, I will give you my two cents worth. Let's talk about the two ways to purchase an annuity first.

- <u>Single Premium-deferred annuity</u> - This type of annuity will allow you to postpone paying taxes on any earnings until you withdraw the money. You can contribute as much money to this type of annuity as you want.

- <u>Immediate Annuities</u> - To purchase this type of annuity, you make a one-time payment. The distributions typically start to pay out within a month after. The deposits income amounts can be fixed or variable and the payments you receive from fixed are based on the amount you have contributed, your age and the dreaded interest rate at time of purchase. The payments will not change

The payment from a variable immediate annuity fluctuate based on the performance of the investment options you have chosen.

Payments may go up or down but they are primarily designed to rise over time to help keep pace with inflation.

FYI - The **principal** in an immediate annuity is not readily accessible. If you need more money than the income provided you can minimize this type of shortcoming by keeping some of your retirement in a savings account or money market fund I suggest the money market fund. You may also lose some of your principal if you choose a certain payout option and then out live it. Fortunately, there are a few different payout options that we will discuss shortly so chill for a minute.

I-BONDS

The I Bond is a pretty straightforward idea. It is sold at face value and grows with inflation protected earnings up to thirty years. I-Bonds are U.S Treasury securities backed by the U.S. Government and you can defer federal taxes on earnings for up to thirty years. They are exempt from state and local income taxes.

I-Bonds usually increase in value every month and interest is compounded semiannually and can be turned into cash anytime after six months. And the best thing is YOU CAN NEVER LOSE MONEY.

CERTIFICATES OF DEPOSIT

Bank CD's require varying initial investments and are a very low risk investment vehicle. They have been very popular in the past with the African-American community because they are safe.

CD's pay at maturity based on a specified time frame (1,2,3 or 5 years). You receive a 1099 tax form at the end of the year and you will incur penalties for early withdrawals.

STOCKS

Stocks are certificates representing ownership in a corporation. In other words, it is pure ownership in a corporation. If the company does well you will earn a dividend. But if the company goes out of business, then you lose your investment.

BONDS

Bonds are certificates representing creditorship in an insurer and issued to raise long-term funds. The holder of the bond is paid interest when due.

INDIVIDUAL RETIREMENT ACCOUNTS

I chose to save what I consider to be one of the best retirement vehicles for last. It's sort of like eating collard greens that second day after they have sat and had a chance to season real good.

That is how I feel about IRAs.

The individual retirement account is a tax deferred retirement account for an individual that permits individuals to set aside two thousand dollars per year with earnings until withdrawals begin. There are two main types of IRA's that we will be discussing; the traditional and the Roth.

TRADITIONAL - The traditional IRA has features that provide the following:

- Deductible or Non Deductible contributions
- Tax deferred growth until distributions begin
- Distributions are taxed as ordinary income
- May make contributions to age 70 1/2 where you must begin taking required minimum distributions (RMD). Usually these distributions must be taken by April 1st of the year after you reach 701/2.

The traditional IRA provides for annual contributions based on your marital status, the year and your income.

MAXIMUM CONTRIBUTION

Year	Contribution	Contribution Over Age 50
2001	$2000.00	$2000.00
2002	3000.00	3500.00
2003	3000.00	3500.00
2004	3000.00	3500.00
2005	4000.00	4500.00
2006	4000.00	5000.00
2007	4000.00	5000.00
2008	5000.00	6000.00

Note - If you are married and filing a joint tax return, a contribution may be made on behalf of a spouse if she is non-working. The total contribution for you and your spouse cannot exceed the income of the working spouse in the year of the contribution.

ROTH

The Roth IRA was established in the Tax Payer Relief Act of 1997. It allows taxpayers that are subject to certain income limits to save for retirement while allowing the savings to grow tax-free. Taxes are paid on contributions but withdrawals are not taxed.

In my opinion the Roth appears to be the better of the two IRA's for the following reasons:

- Normal distributions are forever tax free
- Tax Free withdrawals with no maximum age

- Tax deferred growth
- Earnings are tax free if you hold the account for a minimum of five years and are 59½ years or older when taking withdrawals if you meet special IRS exceptions

Below is the allowable contributions that can be made to a Roth IRA for people filing as joint and single based on their **modified adjusted growth income (MAGI).**

Joint

MAGI	Contribution per person	Contribution over age 50
150k	$3000.00	$3500.00
151k	2700.00	3150.00
152k	2400.00	2800.00
153k	2100.00	2450.00
154k	1800.00	2100.00
155k	1500.00	1750.00
156k	1200.00	1400.00
157k	900.00	1050.00
158k	600.00	700.00
159k	300.00	350.00
160k	0	0

Single

MAGI	Contribution per person	Contribution over age 50
95k	$3000.00	$3500.00
96k	2800.00	3260.00
97k	2600.00	3030.00
98k	2400.00	2800.00
99k	2200.00	2560.00
100k	2000.00	2330.00
101k	1800.00	2100.00
102k	1600.00	1630.00
103k	1400.00	1400.00
104k	1200.00	1400.00
105k	1000.00	1160.00
106k	800.00	930.00
107k	600.00	700.00
108k	400.00	460.00
109k	200.00	230.00
110k	0	0

Note- k denotes thousand

NOTES

CHAPTER FOUR

UNDERSTANDING YOUR
FINANCIAL SELF
Start with what you know and build on what you have
--Kwame Nkrumah

ASK YOURSELF THE THREE W's

When learning how to plan your investment path you must ask yourself:

What do I have?
Whom do I owe?
Where am I in life?

WHAT DO I HAVE?

Like birds flying back to the north from the south in the spring, my mother had a similar ritual duly named spring cleaning. If I close my eyes tightly and listen really closely, I can still hear her voice echoing the words "It's time to see whatcha got" and sometimes I still get a cold chill running down my spine.

Needless to say, the same thing must be done with your financial house as well.

Your Income

This should include all income in your household such as:

- Wages, salary, commissions, pensions, social security child support/alimony, income on real estate and all other income.

Other Assets

- Personal savings, money market funds, money market accounts, CD's, government bonds, mutual funds, stocks, annuities, inheritances and all other assets.

WHOM DO I OWE?

Your Expenses

This should include all debt except the twenty you owe one of the fellas from last week's game of Tunk.

- Taxes, mortgage, food, medical expenses, utilities, telephone, cell phone, car, car maintenance, clothing, childcare, student loans, insurance premiums, home maintenance, hobbies, entertainment, vacations, loans, adult beverages and all other outstanding debts owed.

NOTE - Your total income minus your total expense will provide you with the total dollar amount available for investing. Do not add your other assets to that figure!!!

WHERE AM I IN LIFE?

If you have ever tried to find a house party in the middle of the night, you eventually will utter these magical three words "where am I? " You must ask yourself the same question when determining what stage of your investment life are you currently living and then determine what your goals are for that stage.

Just starting out

Whether you are single or married with or without young children, your cash flow is not yet reached its maximum and you may be living paycheck to paycheck, there are some common goals and objectives to explore such as:

- Saving for a home or condo
- Starting a family
- Saving for transportation
- Educational Savings
- Improving your overall lifestyle

Middle age

Usually, when you are middle age you are middle career and the retirement angel begins to tap you on the shoulder. You should begin to think about it maintaining the quality of your current lifestyle while building your retirement nest egg. These should include

- Increasing income and lowering debt
- Concentrating more on retirement
- Purchasing a new or second car.
- Caring for an elderly parent

Approaching Retirement

These are the years when you are in your prime earning years, all those years of showing up on time, dealing with unruly supervisors and noisy co-workers should finally be paying off. But as you earn more your objectives change yet again:

- Minimizing taxes
- Increasing wealth
- Purchasing a second or summer home
- Assisting children or grandchildren

Retirement

You made it! Now that you no longer want to throw the alarm clock against the nearest wall when it goes off in the morning and the coffee taste just a little bit better your investment objectives enter their final stage. You must consider how to maintain or improve your current lifestyle while making the transition into retirement. Consider the following:

- Having your investments and income keep pace with inflation
- Paying for leisure trips
- Medical expenses
- Increasing estate value
- Maximizing income to meet your living expenses.

While these stages of life are somewhat broad, I hope that you will find one of them similar to your current stage of life.

Now that you have a grasp on investment vehicles and the way they perform, you must first figure out what your objectives are and what type of investor you are? What type of risk are you willing to take? What is your time horizon? An easy way to figure this out by answering the following risk profile analysis. Being as brutally honest with yourself as you possibly can.

YOUR PROFILE

- What are your investment goals?
- Receive current income
- Finance an education\
- Invest for future retirement
- Other

When do you see your investment goals changing?

What investment vehicles best suit your goals?
- I have not made any investments to date.
- CDs or money market instruments
- Mutual Funds
- Stocks
- Bonds
- Annuities
- Real Estate
- 401K Plan

When you hear the term small cap growth or mid-cap value fund, those are share classes. There are four major share classes: Stocks, Bonds, Mutual Funds or Cash & Cash equivalents. These **Asset classes** are a broad category of investments that are available to you, the investor, and broken down as follows:

Large Cap - Stocks or mutual funds that have a market capitalization greater than nine billion dollars, these are some of the largest and most well established companies in the United States.

Small Cap - Stocks or mutual funds with a market capitalization of less than one billion dollars, these are smaller companies and are often new and still developing.

Stocks and Bonds

Cash - Very low risk CD's, commercial paper, money market funds t-bills and cash money.
Mutual Funds- A financial institution whose business is investing other peoples money.

Now for your risk profile and asset allocation quiz:

Time Horizon

When do you expect to start withdrawing money from your investments?
a. Less than 1 year
b. 1-3 years
c. 4-6 years
d. 7-10 years
e. More than 10 years

For how many years do you plan to make withdrawals once they begin?
a. I plan to take a lump sum distribution
b. 1-3 years
c. 4-6 years
d. 7-10 years
e. More than 10 years

Keep in mind that on average a person lives 20-25 years after retirement and will need 70% of the income they earned while working to maintain the same life style.

RISK TOLERANCE

The bigger the risk the bigger the reward is the rule of thumb when considering investments. The following questions will give you an idea of what type of an investor you are, so be honest with yourself.

Which one of the following mixes are you most comfortable with?
a. A high chance of short-term declines in value but with an opportunity for portfolio growth significantly greater than the inflation rate
b. A moderate chance of short-term declines in value in a portfolio that seeks growth that is moderately greater than the inflation rate.
c. A low chance of short-term declines in value but with the chance for portfolio growth slightly greater than the inflation rate.
d. A very low chance of short-term declines in value but with a portfolio that only grows fast enough to keep pace with inflation

I am willing to lose more money in the short term if I can enjoy potentially larger returns in the long term.
a. Strongly agree
b. agree
c. disagree
d. strongly disagree

As mentioned before, the greater the risk, the greater the reward, but also there is a greater risk of loss. The table below displays four hypothetical portfolios over a three year period. Choose the portfolio that best fits you.

Possible Outcomes: $50,000 Invested for 3 years

Option	Worst Case	Best Case
a) Portfolio 1	$40,000	$150,000
b) Portfolio 2	$45,000	$125,000
c) Portfolio 3	$50,000	$100,000
d) Portfolio 4	$60,000	$85,000

What is your investment focus, increasing returns or reducing risk?
a. Increasing returns
b. primarily increasing returns while also reducing risk
c. Primarily reducing risk while also increasing returns
d. Reducing risk

With which investment are you most comfortable?
a. Highest potential long-term return with larger and more frequent intermediate losses
b. Moderate potential long-term return with modest and frequent intermediate losses
c. Lowest potential long-term return with smaller and less frequent intermediate losses.

Consider you invest $50,000 in a portfolio that is expected to have high long-term returns and high short-term risks. The portfolio's value grows to $70,000 in the first year. If your portfolio lost all of its previous gains and some principal in the next month, what would you do?

a. I would not be concerned and would maintain the investment, knowing there continues to be potential for higher long-term returns

b. I would be very concerned and would shift to a slightly more conservative portfolio.

c. I would be very concerned and would shift to a much more conservative portfolio in an attempt to avoid further short term losses

Which investment has the characteristics you favor most?

a. Best chance of meeting long-term goals, may have losses about one out of every three years

b. Good chance of meeting long-term goals, may have losses about one out of every four years

c. Least chance of meeting long-term goals, may have losses about one out of every ten years.

Consider you had an investment showing quarterly returns that had greater short term gain and greater long term loss, but were allocated over a 5 year period. What action would you take?

a. Sell all of the investment immediately and cut my losses

b. Sell some of my investments to reduce exposure to further loss

c. Continue to hold the investments with the expectation of higher returns

Which portfolio below are you most comfortable, given a one year performance with a $50,000 investment?

	Option	Worst case	Best case
a.	Portfolio 1	-20%	+30%
b.	Portfolio 2	-15%	+25%
c.	Portfolio 3	-5%	+15%

CALCULATING YOUR SCORE

Time horizon score

	a	b	c	d	e
1.	0	2	5	8	14
2.	0	1	2	4	7

Time Horizon Total

Risk Tolerance Score

	a	b	c	d
3.	13	9	5	0
4.	9	6	3	0
5.	11	7	4	0
6.	10	7	4	0

7.	10	5	0
8.	10	5	0
9.	11	5	0
10.	0	5	13
11.	13	6	0

WHAT YOUR SCORES MEAN

RISK TOLERANCE SCORE

		0-25	26-75	76-100
T **I** **M** **E**	1-3	**STC**	**STC**	**STC**
E	4-5	**STC**	**STC**	**STC**
H **O** **R** **I**	6-8	**STC**	**STM**	**STA**
Z **O** **N**	9-10	ITC	ITM	ITM
S **C** **O** **R**		ITC	ITM	ITA
E	10 AND UP	LTC	LTM	LTA

84

Explanation of Abbreviations:

STC - Short Term Conservative
STM- Short Term Moderate
STA - Short Term Aggressive
ITC - Intermediate Term Conservative
ITM - Intermediate Term Moderate
ITA- Intermediate Term Aggressive
LTC- Long Term Conservative
LTM- Long Term Moderate
LTA- Long Term Aggressive

(If you have a time horizon of less than one year, these scores are not appropriate for you.)

Now that you have determined what type of investor you are, it is time to choose the investment vehicles that fit your profile. There is no easy way and no get rich quick scheme, you must do your research and become involved in your retirement future, you must run your investment portfolio like a football team performing a two minute drill.

The smallest percentage of every dollar you earn goes toward your retirement, so consider your assets:

Cash
Life Insurance Cash Values
Bonds & Stocks
Retirement Plans
Home
Business
Personal property

In order to plan effectively, you are going to have to inventory your entire financial picture so that you know your complete financial status. Ask yourself, "WHAT DO I OWE AND WHAT DO I OWN?"

CHAPTER FIVE

FOR DA LADIES
save money and money will save you.

In 1979, working wives outnumbered homemakers for the first time in the history of America. The black woman may not have been included in this statistic because she had been working long before the seventies. But as women began entering the workforce, the landscape of investing and retirement planning changed forever.

Women now own their own businesses, hold positions of power in the government, command respect in athletics and still manage to have babies, wipe noses, cook dinners and do most of the child raising in this society.

However, women have managed to live an average of seven years longer than men do and may need more assets accumulated to ensure a comfortable retirement. Women also change jobs more frequently and will often leave the workforce entirely once they give birth. This causes a smaller opportunity to grow a pension. Many women take time off to care for children. They also qualify for less income from social security. For example, the average full monthly benefit for retired female workers based on their own earnings is 62% of the average male.

After I saw the movie *Waiting to Exhale*, I came up with what I called, "The Bernadine

Syndrome," and I find that many women have it. I heard groups of black women discussing the character of Bernadine, and how happy they were when she burned up her unfaithful husband's car and belongings. But she was left in a very precarious situation when he left because he controlled all of the finances and she was the woman being taken care of. Like it or not, nine out of ten women will be responsible for their own finances at some point in their lives. For example:

- Widow
- Divorce
- Recently Graduated from College
- Just Plain Old Single

No matter what the reason, women who do not invest are jeopardizing their future financial security. Because black women have historically faced tremendous obstacles, there is no better time than now to get started. The longer it takes you to get started the more painful it will become. For example, when you first started going to the gym to work your way back into the clothes that you had grown out of, your muscles were sore and you hated it. But as you began to see results, and fit into some of those old clothes, you became more motivated and the exercise became less painful. Your financial fitness is the same way!!! Whether you feel intimidated by the whole thing or not the most important thing you can do is get started now.

A national survey found t
acknowledging the importance of s
majority of women put a higher pri
spending. 54% of women surveyed said   ⎯⎯
more likely to have acquired 30 pairs of shoes
before saving $30,000 in retirement assets.
While eight out of ten single Gen X
women have some retirement savings,

- 53% live paycheck to paycheck
- 75% Say it is more important to look successful
- One out of three would rather talk about their love life than talk to a financial advisor about investing.

Black women face the steepest uphill climb to securing a financial future. Longer life expectancy and lower wages make for a deadly combination if you do not act now. It is imperative that you seek investment and financial planning knowledge with the same zeal that you use when looking for the best sales at the local malls.

You must begin by asking yourself some tough questions, and although the entire book pertains to you, black women have some issues that are unique and must be dealt with accordingly.

I was speaking with a female client who was very anxious to build an investment portfolio. She did not have a lot of money to start but she was committed to starting as soon as possible. As I began to interview her I found that she was thirty nine years old, a criminal defense attorney in her own practice and the proud mother of one adorable son. I also found out that less than 6 months prior to our meeting, she had suffered a heart attack without a financial plan in place. Although it took a catastrophic event for her to see the value in planning for the future, it shouldn't have had to.

Let's take a little test to see how much you know or don't know. So reach inside that Gucci, Coach, Fendi, Dooney & Burke or Nine West andbag and grab a pen. These questions can only help you become a better investor.

1. What percent of women end up managing their own finances at some point in their lives?
a. 10-20%
b. 55-75%
c. 80-90%
d. 95-100%

2. Most women invest their retirement portfolios in:
a. investments that are suitable given their investment profile
b. investments that are too risky
c. investments that are too conservative

3. Most stock market investors get wiped out at least once in their lifetime
a. true
b. false

4 You need a minimum of $ _____ to start investing in mutual funds
a. $25
b. $100
c. $1000
d, $10,000

5. About what percentage of pre-retirement income do many experts say you will need to live comfortably once you have retired?
a. less than 30%
b. 40-50%
c. 60-70%
d. 70-80%
e. more than 80%

6. Over the last 30 years, which investment earned the best return?
a. stocks
b. bonds
c. certificates of deposit (CD's)
d. Savings accounts
e. Money Market funds/accounts

7. Most people who use financial advisors are wealthy.
a. true
b. false

8. If inflation stays at 4% per year, how much would a $50 dinner cost for two in ten years?
a. $54
b. $60
c. $74
d. $80

9. If a person can only afford to invest $50 per month, she shouldn't bother

a. true

b. false

10. Are you ready to make a commitment to yourself?

a. yes

b. no

Answers – 1-C; 2-C; 3-B; 4-A ; 5-D; 6-C; 7-B; 8-C; 9-B; 10-A

Women need to save more than men because of their longer life expectancy. Also, lower paying jobs with little or no pension plans is a concern as well.

Many employers are not required to offer a pension plan; you need to find out if your employer is one of those. Further, you should find out the following about your pension:

What type of plan is it?

There are two basic types of plans; they will be discussed in detail in the next chapter.

Are you included in the plan?

Although an employer may have a plan, they do not have to include every worker, especially one who is part time. Check with your plan administrator for that information.

Do you know what happens if you change jobs or retire early?

If your traditional plan allows you to collect pension benefits before normal retirement age, your benefit may be reduced. Or, if you change jobs and have not worked for a company long enough to qualify, you may lose your pension benefits altogether. Others will allow you to take the money or roll it over into another investment vehicle.

Do you know what happens to your spouse's benefits if he dies before you?

If you are a beneficiary under your spouse's pension plan, you may request a copy of a summary plan description. You may also want to make a written request for certain documents for your records.

Are you entitled to a portion of your spouse's pension if you get divorced?

Men all over the world dread this question, and many would go to great lengths for women not to have access to this information. However, as part of a divorce or legal seperation, you may be able to obtain rights to a portion of your spouse's pension plan. In a private plan, this is done by using a "**qualified domestic relations order (QDRO)**. This is another reason why it is important for you to have documents from your spouse's pension plan administrator, in the event that things go sour in Shangra La. You and your attorney will have the necessary paperwork to determine what requirements will be necessary to meet the needs of the QDRO.

How can I save for retirement if I do not work or have a pension plan?

If you have ever followed a messy Hollywood divorce in the media or read where some professional athlete's wife wants half, it is because of the Bernadine Syndrome: believing that her man will take care of her forever so she doesn't have to take care of herself.

Anyone with compensation or married to someone with compensation can put money into an Individual retirement Account (IRA) or a litany of additional investment vehicles. If you are self-employed you can establish a Simplified Employee Plan

The bottom line is that ladies should get their financial life in order and it can be easier than you think. Between friends, work, the kids and shopping it may be hard to find time to address this all important matter. But the key is to get started and get started NOW.

My mother worked for a cookie factory for about 30 years and retired at the young age of 63. Her company did not offer a 401(k) retirement plan until she was 5 years from retirement which did not give her much time to participate. However she was included in the company's old plan which after many years of service provided her with a gold watch and a pension based on her years of service. That along with her social security and the fact that my dad is still alive and has his retirement from the union and social security, they live a comfortably, modest life. The good news is that they were lucky. Not all that toil in someone else's factory has a pension, especially women.

For several decades, women have increased their earning power and financial independence. That, along with watching Oprah Winfrey, has given women a tremendous amount of progress. But when it comes time to taking control of finances, there is still a long way to go. Today, 46% of the work force is made up of women so you no longer have to feel alone when you roll out of bed in the morning. Further, more than 40% of all wealthy Americans are women.

Still, 75% of our elderly poor are female!! That should be a huge wake up call and despite many advances, women remain less prepared to provide for their financial future than their male counterparts. Women not only start saving and investing later, they are saving less, either by necessity or because the mall is calling. Let's be real. Women are putting marriage and family on hold in pursuit of career goals at records rates. Divorce is at an all time high and there are more black families with a woman as head of household than ever before in the history of this country.

Women often are forced into taking control of their finances in the wake of some crisis such as divorce, illness, unemployment, or death of a spouse. This forces them to make decisions as the whirlwind of stress and emotion may be spiraling out of control. After countless interviews and surveys, the number one reason women are hesitant to invest is the fear of the unknown. Many women start out investing too conservatively or putting their money in the wrong investment altogether and not realizing the type of return they should have.

With all of those hurdles, let not your heart be troubled. Taking charge of your financial future is easier than you think. You don't have to be an expert. As a matter of fact, you don't have worry about it. Your first step may be to simply talk to an advisor. If you don't know of one, ask a friend or family member or you can always call me.

As I mentioned earlier, I don't want you to stop consuming, I just want you to become a better consumer. The five basic steps that you need to get started are as follows:

1. Make Your Financial Future a Priority
2. Get Started Now!!!
3. Seek Good Advice
4. Become More Educated
5. Don't Worry

Although women have become such a diverse group in our culture, the financial concerns remain consistent with one another. I have profiled six women. As you read their stories, ask yourself if any of these women are you or someone you know.

Case #1- Faye

Bio - 36 years old, married, one child, self-employed, $40,000 annual income.

Her own words – *"I never really thought about my financial future or retirement much. I grew up believing that you grow up, you get married and you work hard to provide for yourself and your family but the husband would take care of that stuff.*

It is strange that I was willing to turn over my finances to my husband for management and he worked for the post office and I wasn't willing to sit down and talk to a professional."

Faye's goal was to retire by fifty-five, travel, and only work if she wanted to. For her, that was financial freedom.

Case #2- Emma

Bio - 53 year old, married, no kids at home, school teacher.

Her own words – *"I always thought that we were saving enough. I paid the bills and my husband made the decisions regarding our retirement, but when he was diagnosed with Alzheimer's, I was forced to make financial decisions I was not accustomed to making. I found out that we were going to fall short of our retirement goals and with my husband needing full time medical care, our retirement income was being depleted. I wish I had become more involved ten years ago."*

Emma is now facing an uphill battle that may force her into financial ruin. Because Americans are living longer even with illnesses such as Alzheimer's, the expenses will mount and she may outlive her retirement income.

Case #3- Bernadine

Bio - 45 years old, three kids, homemaker, divorced.

Her own words – *"I thought that we would be married forever; I was educated and had done what I considered to be the right things in life. When I got married, my husband did not want me to work, and he was a good provider. When the kids started arriving being the best wife and mother I could be became my full time job. I never worried about my financial future. But after the divorce, I had to enter the workforce much later and life and with all of the new financial responsibilities I have, saving for retirement seems like a pipe dream."*

Bernadine is facing a problem that is becoming more and more frequent, but all is not lost for her. With a sound financial plan Bernadine can achieve her goals.

Case #4 - Shanene

Bio - 26 year old, single, two kids, $24, 000 annual income, access to 401(k) plan

Her own words – *"All my decisions in life have not been good ones, but I am glad I have my kids and I love them. One of my children's father is unemployed and provides no child support. The other pays support through the court system but it is not that much. I would like to go back to school and purchase a home some day. But with all of my bills, I am barely making ends meet. I have not started making contributions to my 401k yet and I don't see how I can afford to."*

Shanene must embrace the concept of paying herself first, and seeking information that will help her reach her goals. There are many programs that she will qualify for but it will take commitment and diligence.

Case # 5 – Jennifer

Bio – 31 year, single, employed, college graduate $50,000 annual income

Her own words – *"I put a little in my 401k because it seemed like I should, but I will admit that my retirement is one of the last things on my mind, I shop a lot and I have a very nice car and I live in a condo. Retirement seems so far off and I can worry about that later. Besides, I don't understand all that stuff."*

Jennifer is in the perfect position to really accomplish a bulletproof financial plan, but if she doesn't act now she will look up and ten years will have passed and time is something none of us can get back.

Case #6 – Shirley

Bio – 62 year old, retired, homemaker, widowed

Her own words – *"I thought that being a homemaker my whole life made me one of the lucky ones, but in my generation, many woman did not work. My husband took care of all of the finances and we did fine. When he died, I didn't know how his pension worked and what I was entitled to receive. I had no social security benefits and it took a while to receive any of his. Thank God the house was paid for, I now live on a very fixed income and my monthly expenses exceed that income. I wish I knew what to do."*

Shirley is a growing segment of the population that society would rather forget about, but even Shirley has options to make her lifestyle better.

The preceding profiles have been a collection of women I have sat and talked with. If you recognize any of them, tap them on the shoulder and get them pointed in the right direction. I hope that this chapter has been beneficial to you. Along with the other information contained in this book, you are now well on your way to building a financial strategy and achieving your financial goals.

CHAPTER SIX

RETIREMENT PLANS
The ant stores up during the summer, knowing
that a time will come when he will need the resources

Although there are many retirement plans, statistics show the majority of Black Americans participate in two plans the 401k plan and the 403b plan, and those are the two plans we will discuss in detail.

401K PLAN

From its inception over twenty years ago, the 401k plan has gained steam as it replaced the old traditional pension plan. But it was not until the decade of the nineties that black Americans began contributing in record numbers. If you will notice, it was not until then that the 401k reached new levels of growth. The 401k has provided a vast majority of black Americans the best opportunity to accumulate wealth for retirement.

The 401k plan was named after a section of the tax code and is a federally approved plan that allows you to set aside a percentage of your pay before taxes are taken out. All growth in your 401k is tax deferred. However, once the money is in your 401k plan, you generally cannot take it out until you reach the age of

591/2, except for some special circumstances such as health emergencies, education and purchasing a home.

GETTING STARTED

There is a very old saying, "look before you leap." Although the percentage of black Americans participating in 401k plans has increased, it is still a very small percentage overall and the primary reason does not appear to be lack of income, but lack of knowledge.

Become familiar with your company's 401k plan. Request a <u>Summary Plan Description</u>. By law your employer must provide you with this. Plan Description. The Summary Plan describes:

- Eligibility (usually you are eligible to join a 401k plan if are 21 years of age and have worked with the company for a certain period of time)
- Vesting
- Benefit Payouts
- Funds Available
- Who holds the 401k assets

In order to make the most of your 401k and to make the best decisions, you need to know that information as well as the following

- What is the maximum amount/percentage you can contribute?
- What is the percentage your employer will match?
- How many years of company service are required before you are fully vested in your employer's contribution to your 401k?
- How often can you transfer money between the investment options in your plan?
- What are your investment options?

Based on the plan that your employer has sponsored, your 401k plan can have many benefits:

Company Matching Funds- Most employers will match your contribution dollar for dollar up to a certain percent and then you are on your own. Most matches vary between 2%-6%.

Tax Deferred Growth- As I mentioned earlier, your dollars will not be taxed as long as they grow and remain in your 401k plan. This allows your account balance to grow more quickly.

Control-Primarily you can choose how you want your dollars invested.

Your Current gross income is reduced by the amount you contribute - Contributions to your 401k plan are usually made pre-tax, which means you do not pay federal or state tax (in most cases) until the money is withdrawn, that means you have more money in your account working for you today.

Portability-If you leave your current employer, you can take your money with you.

Now with all of the events leading up to the tragedy of 9/11 you may be wondering, "is my 401k ok?" For the first time in nearly twenty years, the most popular retirement plan in the American workplace lost money and people saw their dreams of comfortable retirement begin to get further and further away. Before you find yourself having sleepless nights or you consider taking hostages, rest easy. It is still possible to achieve your retirement goals and quite possibly make your 401k plan stronger.

NEW TAX LAWS

Like well-trained soldiers, new tax laws marched in with the year 2002 and some of those law's will directly affect your 401k plan. For example: maximum contributions in the calendar year were $10,500, the limit for 2002 is $11,000 and will increase by $1000 per year continuing to 2006 where it will level off at $15,000. The good news is this, if you are in a 401k plan and you have managed to reach the tender age of fifty, you will have the privilege of making additional contributions ($1000 in 2002 and will increase to $5000 by 2006). This is known as "the catch-up provision. For those of you who read this book, fondly remember playing eight track tapes and taking pictures in those big wicker chairs at the Isley Brothers concert and for whatever reason you have gotten off to a late start toward building your nest egg, this type of news should be rather exciting.

Throughout the 1990s, 401k plans could do no wrong, but with corporate fraud and bankruptcy becoming as common as the flu in December, visions of working longer than you planned or maybe having to start a second career once you retire have replaced that vision of leisure retirement lifestyle.

In order to stay or get on track, you are going to have to take some steps to make that happen. I affectionately refer to this as my "Triple R Attack"

Review

Go get all of those shoe boxes and over stuffed file folders and look at your retirement plan statements and bank statements. Ask yourself:

- How much do I have in my retirement plan?
- What amount is my company matching?
- Has my retirement goals changed?

- What are my investment options?
- How do I have my investment dollar divided?

Answering these questions is the first step to getting back on the road to those Mai Tais on the beach.

<u>Reallocate</u>

As mentioned earlier, in the 1990s many did well in the investment market and most took the position of "if it aint broke don't fix it," but with the collapse of the dot com industry and the tech market having the wind knocked out of it, you may need to take a look at where your money is invested and if you are still on target to meet your retirement goals. If you are not, then you may have to reallocate some of your funds to different investment vehicles. In other words clean house, get those non-performing funds out and replace them with funds that are performing, while considering the following:

- What type of investor have I become?
- What budget commitment can I make every month? (long term success in the market consist of time in the market, not timing the market).
- Do I know an investment professional that I can meet with to assist me with this?

That third question is a big one. As I mentioned earlier, blacks have a greater opportunity to build wealth through 401k plans than ever before and many have done well, but as the market turned downward, instead of seeking professional assistance many blacks became as protective as prisoners in the pen at dinner time. From my personal experience, the mentality is, "if it is going to be lost, I will lose it on my own".

I urge you all to at least talk to a professional. You go to the doctor when you have an ache and to a lawyer if you have to go to court. But with something as important as your financial future, you do not seek out a professional. Any financial advisor worth his salt will review this information at no cost.

React

DO IT NOW!

Privatizing a portion of your retirement

With all of the corporate scandals, it proves that there are less than honorable men in the world and many have fallen victim to having all of their retirement eggs in one basket. For example: *Rick believed so much in the future of his employer of almost 30 years, that he put all of his 401k funds in company stock. He also purchased shares of his company stock as part of a stock option plan. In addition, he received some 15,000 shares in company stock as a gift as well as stock contributions the company matched in his 401k plan.*

Rick, a 67-year-old retired employee living in the Midwest, owns between 25,000 and 26,000 shares of company stock. At the end of 2001, it was worth about 2 million dollars. It is now worth less than $10,000.

Rick says now that the worst mistake was not diversifying his retirement funds into other investments.

There are literally thousands of stories like that, but you do not have to be one of them. I am a big believer in controlling a portion of your own destiny, which insulates you from your company going bankrupt or being sold or some COO disappearing in the middle of the night with the company retirement.

Open your own Roth or traditional IRA or any number of other investment vehicles where you and you alone hold the key to the lock.

Don't misunderstand me, the 401k plan can be a tremendous retirement vehicle. If your company provides a match it should be your primary retirement vehicle. It just should not be your only one.

403B RETIRMENT PLAN

If you are an educator, minister, doctor or nurse working in a hospital or an employee of any non-profit organization you must participate in a 403b retirement plan. These plans may also be called Tax-Deferred Annuities (TDA) or Tax-Sheltered Annuities (TSA). A 403B plan is similar to a 401k plan in that it is also named after a section of the IRS code and the money that you contribute to the plan grows tax deferred. The plan may allow for loans, and contributions can be payroll deducted. It also has catch-up provisions built into it. That is just about where the similarities end.
There are two basic types of 403b plans:

1. Erisa - The employer matches your contribution up to a certain percentage
2. Non-Erisa - There is no match

Investments in a 403b plan by law are limited to two categories: annuities and mutual funds. The reason for this law is simple. A company that offers a 401k plan is for profit and may offer stock or stock options. But there is no stock to buy in a non-profit organization. Although you are limited to those two types of investments, you still have a broad range of investment choices.

The biggest draw back in 403b plans are the surrender charges if you want to take your money out of the plan for a non emergency. This could drastically reduce your 403b plan funds and it causes many to remain in a plan that is not performing well or not being serviced well for fear of losing money if they get out of the plan. Further, the money in a 403b plan can never be rolled into a 401k plan, however, it can be rolled into an IRA.

IRS RULING 90-24

For many years, school teachers and other participants felt trapped in their 403b plans with no way out until IRS Rule 90-24, which allows direct, tax-free transfers between 403b funding vehicles. This specifically applies to 403(b) plans.

This ruling enables participants of 403(b) plans to have more control over their investments. Even if an employer does not allow a particular carrier to do business, the employee may want to invest in some of that carrier's funds. Through 90-24, the employee can move as much of his or her money as desired to another carrier. Even though you may be subject to a surrender charge, you could take advantage of the free out to transfer 10% at a time. If you are in a bad plan, it will be worth it. The reason for transferring money out of your current plan in 10% increments is because most plans allow you to take 10% out without surrender fees. Prior to this ruling you would have had to exchange your entire contract to a new one. If you are in a non-erisa plan you do not need an employers consent to transfer your money, and you would suffer no tax consequences for the transfer.

Even though this ruling allows 403b participants more opportunities to accumulate wealth, your current 403b provider would prefer that you not know about this ruling. He wants you to keep your money under his control!

Always ask questions of your plan provider. When participating in a company sponsored plan, remember to diversify your dollars, have an understanding of your investment options, and privatize a portion of your retirement.

<u>NOTES</u>

CHAPTER SEVEN

COLLEGE PLANNING
*The Masses must move, but it must be the classes
that move them.*

For anyone that has received a call from a bill collector at work harassing you over your student loans, I know you do not want to put your children through that nightmare. Statistics show that black children remain far behind other ethnic groups when it comes to a college education.

Over the course of the last twenty years, the cost of a college education has increased by nearly twice the rate of inflation. And it is likely that the cost of higher education will continue to rise. Every parent or guardian would like their children to have better in life than they did. Although you can never place a price tag on the quality of someone's future, one of the simple truths is that a college education (or at least acquiring a secondary education that will provide you with in-demand technical skills,) will provide an advantage in the work force.

The average cost of a four-year undergraduate education at a public university is $51,618. That cost could be double at private colleges, such as Morehouse or Spelman. A child born in the year 2002, with a rate of only 5% to the academic year of 2021 will possibly pay up to $124,225.

Although many black students rely on financial aid, there simply will not be enough to go around, and bear in mind, 60% of all financial aid is in the form of loans that must be repaid at some point. As black Americans, we must rely on ourselves to educate our black children.

Although college enrollment among blacks is up, many often run out of financial resources before completing their undergraduate studies. As this trend continues, the argument can be made that this has a direct link to the socio-economic status of black America as a whole.

I had the good fortune of conducting a seminar with a group of inner city high school students from a predominately black high school and I asked them the question. "What would you do with a million dollars?" Although the answers varied, there were two common denominators:

1. They would put money away for school
2. Spend, Spend, Spend!!!

I don't know if they wrote number one for my benefit or not, but it proves that black youths are thinking about furthering their education. Since I did require them to put their name on their answers, the best response that I received was, "A million dollars is a large amount of money, so there is a large number of things I'd do with it. I would probably buy me some new clothes (about $10,000 worth). I'd then buy 3 or 4 cars for my family and myself (approx $100,000). I would pay for the full repair of my church (approx $40,000) and for some renovations (approx $30,000). I'd buy my family a new house (approx $125,000). Then I would invest the rest and let it accumulate." I found this to be both surprising and encouraging that a child with an imaginary million dollar windfall understands the need to invest.

The concept of investing is still lacking in black children and many adults. It simply isn't discussed at the dinner table and just like building a portfolio, the sooner you start the better.

Whether it be vocational or technical school, public or private undergraduate programs, professional schools, or Graduate school, the time to start preparing is right now. Following are six ways you can invest in your child's college education:

TRADITIONAL & ROTH IRA's

This is a retirement account in which contributions grow tax free and withdrawals can be made for education.

Tax implications - traditional: penalty-free withdrawals for education but taxable at account owners tax rate. Roth: Tax-free principal withdrawals and penalty free use of earnings for education.

Financial aid implications - Retirement assets are not typically considered part of financial calculations.

Contribution limits - $3000 annual contribution, $6000 annual contribution per couple (effective 2002) a catch-up provision is available for those fifty and older

Estate planning implications – none.

Advantages - account owner controls assets. Children can open and fund an account with earned income.

Disadvantages-Withdrawals reduce tax-advantage retirement savings.

SERIES EE BONDS

These are government bonds that provide guaranteed tax-deferred interest.

Tax implications - tax deferred growth.

Financial aid implications - they are the assets of the student.

Contribution limits - no limit.

Estate Planning Implications - none.

Advantages - guaranteed minimum return.

Disadvantages - Series EE bonds provide a low rate of return, the tax benefits phase out for high income households and earnings are taxable when HOPE or Lifetime Learning Credit is used.

UTMA/UGMA ACCOUNTS

These are Custodial accounts in which securities are invested on behalf of the child.

Tax implications - a portion of the earnings are taxable at a minor's rate, which is lower.
Financial aid implications-the assets are considered those of the child which can have a higher impact of financial aid calculations.
Contribution limits - no limit.
Estate planning implications - If contributions larger than $10,000 are made annually it may be subject to a gift tax.
Advantages - there are no income restrictions and an account can be established by anyone
Disadvantages - the earnings are taxable and minors gain control of the assets at age 18 and can use the assets for any purpose. So if you have a child that may change his mind this may not be the investment account for you.

COVERDELL EDUCATION SAVINGS ACCOUINT

This was formerly known as the education IRA in which contributions grow tax free.
Tax implications - tax-free earnings
Financial aid implications - As with the UGMA/UTMA, the assets are the minors and could have a higher impact on financial aid calculations.

Contribution limits - $2000 maximum annual contribution and there are income restrictions for higher income households.

Estate planning implications - none.

Advantages - Anyone can establish an account and if not used by one child the funds can be transferred to another child. These funds can be used for elementary and secondary education expenses including public, private and religious schools.

Disadvantages - The contributions are low, there is a 10% penalty for non-education related withdrawals and earnings are taxable when used with HOPE or Lifetime Learning Credit is used.

PREPAID TUTION PLAN

Contributions are made to specific in-state schools to lock into future tuition at selected schools at today's rates.

Tax implications - tax-deferred earnings and withdrawals are taxed at the rate of the student.

Financial Aid implications - withdrawals reduce financial aid.

Contribution limits - maximum contributions vary from state to state.

Estate planning implications - there is no federal gift tax on contributions for each beneficiary and the value gifted is excluded from the estate.

Advantages - there are no income restrictions

and anyone can establish an account

Disadvantages - Use may not be transferable to out-of-state schools. The account owner has no control over investments and there is a 10% penalty for non-qualified withdrawals.

529 COLLEGE SAVINGS PLAN

I have saved the best for last. The 529 college savings is by far the most comprehensive of all of the college savings plans. These plans are state sponsored so contributions may vary; however contributions are invested and grow federal tax free and offers maximum flexibility on many levels.

Tax implications - tax-free earnings

Financial Aid implications -a lower weighing is given in many financial aid calculations because the assets belong to the account owner and not the student. Further, you may have penalty-free withdrawals up to the amount of any scholarship if the student receives a scholarship.

Contribution limits - up to $251,000 per beneficiary depending on your state.

Estate planning implications - no federal gift tax on lump sum contributions of up to $100,000 per couple filing jointly. The value gifted is excluded from estate taxes.

Advantages -high contribution limits, no income restrictions, account can be established by anyone, account owner controls assets. Beneficiary can be changed at any time and the funds can be used for a broad range of education related expenses.

Disadvantages - 10% penalty for non-qualified withdrawals.

Keep in mind the 529 plan is a state sponsored plan, and the deductions may be unlimited in that state. For example if you were to choose a 529 plan, outside of the state that you reside you may not be eligible for tax breaks available in that state. Below is a list of the 529 plans and the states that sponsor them:

Alabama

Higher Education 529 Fund
Mutual Fund Company-Van Kampen
(866) 529-2228
www.treasury.state.al.us/

Alaska

T Rowe Price 529 Plan
Mutual Fund Company - T Rowe Price
(800) 369-3641
www.Troweprice.com

Arizona

Arizona Family College Savings Plan
Mutual Fund Company-Securities Management and Research
(888) 667-3239
www.smrinvest.com

InvestEd
Mutual Fund Company- Waddell & Reed
(888) 923-3355
www.waddellReed.com

Arkansas

Gift College Investment Plan
529 Provider-Franklin Templeton Investment
Company
(877) 615-4116
www.thegiftplan.com

California

Golden State Scholar Share College Savings
Trust
529 Provider-Tiaa Creff
(877) 728-4338
www.scholarshare.com

*Colorado

College Invest Scholars Choice College Saving
Plan
529 Provider-Citi Group
(800) 478-5651 or (888) 572-4652
www.scholars-choice.com

Connecticut

Conneticut Higher Education Trust (chet)
529 Provider-Tiaa Creff
(888) 799-2438
www.aboutchet.com

Delaware

Delaware College Investment Plan
529 Provider-Fidelity Investments
(800) 544-1655
www.fidelity.com

District of Columbia

DC 529 College Savings Plan
529 Provider-Calvert Asset Management
Res. (800) 987-4859 Non-Res (800) 368-2745
www.dccollegesavings.com

Florida

Florida College Investment Plan
529 Provider- Northern Trust Company, Trust
Company Capital Management, U.S. Trust Asset
Management, Deutsche Asset manangement
(800) 552-4723
www.florida529plans.com

Georgia

Higher Education Savings Plan
529 Provider-Tiaa Creff
(877) 424-4377
www.gacollegesavings.com

Hawaii

Tuition Edge
529 Provider-Delaware Investments
(866) 529-3343
www.tuitionedge.com/tuitionedge/

Idaho

Idaho College Savings Plan (Ideal)
529 Provider-Tiaa Creff
(866) 433-2533
www.idsaves.com

+*Illinois

Bright Start College Savings Plan
529 Provider-Citi Group
(877) 432-7444
www.brightstartsavings.com

+Indiana

College Choice
529 Provider-One Group Investments
(866) 400-7526
www.collegechoiceplan.com

Iowa

College Savings Iowa
529 Provider-Vanguard
(888) 672-9116
www.collegesavingsiowa.com

Kansas

Learning Quest Education Savings
529 Provider-American Century Investments
(800) 579-2203
www.learningquestsavings.com

+Kentucky

Kentucky Education Savings Trust
529 Provider-Tiaa Creff
(877) 598-7878
www.kysaves.com

$Louisiana

Start Saving Plan
529 Provider-State of Louisiana Treasury
(800) 259-5626
www.osfa.state.la.us

Maine

Next Generation College Investing Plan
529 Provider-Merrill Lynch
(877) 463-9843
www.nextgenplan.com

Maryland

College Savings Plan of Maryland
529 Provider-T Rowe Price
(888) 463-4723
www.collegesavingsmd.com

Massachusetts

U Fund College Investing Plan
529 Provider-Fidelity Investments
(800) 544-2776
www.fidelity.com

$Michigan

Michigan Education Savings Program
529 Porvider-Tiaa Creff
(877) 861-6377
www.misaves.com

$Minnesota

Minnesota College Savings Plan
529 Provider-Tiaa Creff
(877) 338-4646
www.mnsaves.com

Mississippi

Mississippi Prepaid Affordable College Tuition
(Impact)
529 Provider-Tiaa Creff
(800) 987-4450
www.treasury.state.ms.us/impact.htm

Missouri

Missouri Saving For Tuition Program (Mo$t)
529 Provider-Tiaa Creff
(888) 414-6678
www.missourimost.org/

Montana

Pacific Funds 529 College Savings Plan
529 Provider-Pacific Funds
(800) 888-2723
www.pacificlife.com

Nebraska

College Savings Plan Of Nebraska (Neb529)
529 Provider-Union Bank and Trust
(888) 993-3746
www.planforcollegenow.com

Additional providers-Aim Funds, State Farm,
T.D. Waterhouse.

Nevada

American Skandia College Savings Program
529 Provider-American Skandia
(800) 752-6342
www.americanskandia.com

Additional 529 providers:

USSA - (800) 645-6288
Vanguard- (866) 734-4530
Columbia Funds- (877) 994-2529
Strong Capital Management- (877) 529-5295

New Hampshire

Fidelity Advisor 529 Plan
529 Provider-Fidelity Investments
(800) 522-7297
www.fidelity.com

Additional 529 plan
Unique College Investing Plan
(800) 544-1722

New Jersey

NJBest 529 College Savings Plan
529 Provider-Franklin Templeton
(877) 465-2378
www.njbest.com

*New Mexico

The Education Plans College Savings
529 Provider-State Street Global
(877) Ed Plan8
www.theeducationplan.com/investments/7_2jsp

Additional Providers:
Oppenheimer- (866) 529-7283
New York Life- (866) 529-7367

+New York

New York College Savings Plan
529 Provider- Note: as of 07/30/2003 the Tiaa
Creff contract has expired and the Vanguard
Upromise College Saving Plan is the new plan.
(877) 697-2837
www.nysaves.com

North Carolina

National College Savings Plan
529 Provider-Met Life
(800) 600-3453
www.cfnc.org

North Dakota

College Save
529 Provider-Bank of North Dakota
(866) 728-3529
www.collegesave4u.com

Ohio

Ohio College Advantage Savings Plan
529 Provider- Ohio Tuition Trust Authority and
Putnam Investment Management
(800) 233-6734
www.collegeadvantage.com

Oklahoma

Oklahoma College Savings Plan
529 Provider-Tiaa Creff
(877) 654-7284
www.ok4saving.com

Oregon

Oregon College Savings Plan (facts 529)
529 provider-Strong and First American Funds
(866) 772-8464
www.estrong.com

Additional provider:
Mfs- (866) 637-7526

+Pennsylvania

Tap 529 Investment Plan
529 Provider-Delaware Investments
(800) 440-4000
www.tap529.com

Rhode Island

CollegeBound Fund
529   Provider-AllianceBernstein   Investment
Research and Management
(888) 324-5057
www.collegeboundfund.com

Additional Provider:
J.P. Morgan- (877) 576-3529

*South Carolina

Future Scholar 529 College Savings Plan
529 Provider-Bacap Distributors, LLC
(888) 244-5674
www.futurescholar.com
Tennessee

Best Savings Plan
529 Provider-Tiaa Creff
(888) 486-2378
www.tnbest.com

Texas

Tomorrows College Investment Plan
529 Provider-Enterprise Capital Management
(800) 445-4723
www.enterprise529.com

Utah

Utah Educational Savings Plan (UESP)
529 Provider-Vanguard
(800) 418-2551
www.uesp.org

Vermont

Vermont Higher Education Investment Plan
529 Provider-Tiaa Creff
(800) 637-5860
www.vsac.org

+Virginia

Virginia Education Savings Trust (Vest)
529 Provider-State of Virginia
(888) 567-0540
www.virginia529.com

College America
529 Provider-American Funds
(800) 421-4120
www.Americanfunds.com

Washington

Guaranteed Education Tuition (GET)
529 Provider- State of Washington Investment
Board
(877) 438-8848
www.get.wa.gov

*West Virginia

Smart 529 College Savings Option
529 Provider-The Hartford
(866) 574-3542
www.hartfordinvestor.com/products/collegesp.htm

Wisconsin

Edvest
529 Provider-Strong Capital Management
(888) 338-3789
www.estrong.com

Wyoming

College Achievement Plan
529 Provider-Mercury Funds and MFS
(877) 529-2655
www.collegeachievementplan.com

I encourage you to research these plans to discover which one will best fit your needs. The 529 plan provider, the state tax benefits and any state that may have special matching feature are all things to consider before making this important decision.

A sound education is the cornerstone of success, and although it will not fully neutralize the hurdles that African-Americans face in the workforce it will definitely empower us as a race and create a more competitive environment in the workforce.

CHAPTER EIGHT

INVESTMENT STRATEGIES
Without a roadmap, any path will take you there

Investing is built on a simple concept called Time Value of Money.

Money received today is worth more than the same amount received in the future For example, if you invest a dollar in a savings account at your bank paying 3% annual interest, at the end of one year, the dollar would have grown to $1.03. The initial dollar would be referred to as the present value. The 3% represents the interest rate and the term is for one year. The $1.03 equals the future value. The interest earned ($0.03) is the reward for delaying using that dollar for one year into the future.

Present Value(PV) =$1.00
Future Value(FV) =$1.03
Interest = $0.03

PAY YOURSELF FIRST! The experts say you should pay yourself 10% of your paycheck, but for a lot of us that is not realistic. Do not short change yourself, but pay yourself as much as you can and be consistent.

So, get ready to become fully engaged in understanding how to get from zero to retirement with money to live. Investing is the practice of delayed gratification.

I want to say that one more time, "INVESTING IS THE PRACTICE OF DELAYED GRATIFICATION."

Often I have been sitting in a bar or in the barbershop and the topic of what I do for a living comes up and almost always, the question is "how fast can I get rich?" It's true that some people have literally made millions overnight, but I would bet you that the list that have lost millions overnight is a much longer list. Creating an investment strategy is a long term endeavor, it is not a sprint. It is a leisurely stroll and if you do it correctly you will even enjoy the scenery.

Wealth management goes far beyond just building wealth Although building wealth is important, preserving wealth and wealth distribution are just as important.

The experts say that 92% of a successful portfolio is asset allocation.

Proper asset allocation will allow you to diversify your portfolio, thereby allowing you to realize maximum performance. Read your prospectus, become engaged in the building of your portfolio. If you have mutual funds, look at the top ten holdings and the fund mangers objectives, and make sure they are in line with your objectives. When building a portfolio, one of your goals will be to keep your mutual fund overlap at 10% or less. This is considered to be a diversified portfolio.

By diversifying your assets, you avoid the risk of having all your money concentrated in just one type of investment. Asset allocation works because different investments perform well at different times. But good or bad, stay in. You may switch funds, but stay engaged in the market. Stocks have posted negative returns in eleven different years since 1950. In those years, bonds achieved positive returns in ten of the eleven years. So although you may have to modify your portfolio continue to work your plan.

When it comes to building your investment portfolio, there is no "one size fits all." Your plan has to fit your needs only. Once you figure out what type of investor you are, you are ready to build your portfolio and become more involved in your financial future.

As an investor you should take seven financial concerns into consideration. Ask yourself the following:

1. How important is it for me to own assets that seek to maintain their purchasing power by keeping pace with inflation?
2. How concerned am I about getting all the tax relief to which I am legally entitled, that is both suitable and logical for me?
3. Do I feel a need for assets that can be quickly converted to cash, in the event of an accident, illness, disability or unexpected death
4. How concerned am I about having guaranteed savings; that I will not lose any investment when it is time for retirement?

5. Am I concerned about receiving maximum current income from investment assets, rather than growth value?

6. In the event of death, what is my concern that your investment portfolio not cause a tax burden for your loved ones left behind?

7. Why am I investing? For a home, a second home, retirement, or college?

THE LAYAWAY THEORY

When I was about nine years old, I heard this magical term that I had never heard before. It had the promise of making all of Christmas dreams come true. My mom and I were in a K-Mart department store and I was running the store showing her everything that I wanted Santa to deliver to me on Christmas morning.

As I began pointing out the GI Joe with the Kung Fu grip, the Tyco race car set, the Huffy bicycle, the Stretch Armstrong and everything else imaginable, I overheard my mother whisper to my aunt, "I can put it on lay-a-way."

The lay-a-way has been a friend to black America for many years. It has allowed Black America to increase its purchasing power. Furthermore, the lay-a-way has allowed for little black kids to have wonderful Christmas seasons, Easter suits and school clothes. I speak of the lay-a-way with such glee and vigor because the concept is simple and effective.

When you roll that basket full of goodies to the back of the store and the clerk rings up the total of $568.22 and you look into your wallet and only see twenty dollars, something very important happens. An agreement is made. You agree to pay a small portion and they will hold the merchandise you have presented with the promise to give it to you in the future when you have paid the entire balance.

Because black Americans were not able to get credit cards or open an account at the department stores as easily as our white counterparts, the lay-a-way was the way to somewhat level the playing field.

The very concept of investing in a mutual fund or a life insurance policy or overall financial planning is very close to the same theory. You agree to give a small amount per month to a mutual fund with the end goal of reaching retirement with a certain amount there waiting to be handed to you. So before you run out and lay-a-way that big screen television or Rolex watch or new pair of anything, invest in your future. Invest in yourself. As black Americans, let's embrace the lay-a-way theory and begin growing wealth.

ORGANIC INVESTING

Webster's Dictionary defines organic as "something organized or systematically arranged." When you create a portfolio that addresses all of your financial concerns, I like to call this organic investing.

I've heard it said of Black America that we have a store front mentality. If we can't walk in the store and see the goods we will not purchase the goods. We as black Americans must release the store front mentality; it has kept us three steps behind for eternity. Believe it or not, the bank is not your only or best option.

I want you to close your eyes, pretend like you are in church at Altar call. Close your eyes and name as many places that you can think of to invest your money. Now ask yourself, "was my bank the first thing that popped into my head?" Organic investing does not include a savings account at the bank. It is time to cut the apron strings of "Mother Bank" and begin to utilize all vehicles available to you that will help you create and build wealth.

Organic investing must reach beyond investing in the stock market or mutual funds. Black America must begin recycling black dollars in our own communities, our own businesses and our own neighborhoods. Statistics show that a dollar is recycled seven times in the Jewish community before it leaves that community, the Asian dollar is recycled at least 4 times before it makes its exit from the community. But the black dollar recycles itself zero times. Think about how often you drive by black businesses to get to the *big* mall on the other size of town.

As I mentioned earlier, I do not want you to stop purchasing. I want you to purchase better! Of every dollar that you spend, ask yourself, "is this a good investment? Or can I make a better purchase?" I look at the black celebrities that have earned a tremendous amount of money only to lose it all, be forced into bankruptcy, or die in poverty - Toni Braxton, TLC, Silk, Red Foxx, Sammy Davis Jr.- just to name a few.

If you take nothing else from this book, take this: expand your mind, and consider a strategic plan that you create. Equip yourself with all the information that you can get your hands on and realize that just because you can't walk into the store front doesn't mean that it isn't worth it.

Consider all avenues that are made available to you. We all had that grandmother who taught us to keep a little cash stash in the house. However, the stakes are so much higher now and it's time for us to get in the game and play it to win. Invest! Invest! Invest!!!!!

For a while I specialized in retirement plans for non-profit organizations (403b plans). This put me on the front lines of the inner city school districts in Atlanta, Georgia. I saw firsthand what some of these young men and women are facing. I was speaking to one of the educators in a high school and I made the comment, "when I was in school, we behaved like teenagers but we still wanted to learn. These children have no interest in becoming educated."

Her response was that the children she attempts to educate do not have proper diet, proper clothing and other core socio-economic needs that the majority of people take for granted. With a Black America as wealthy and prosperous as the one we live in, I find this to be a travesty.

If I sound a little angry its because I am. We as black Americans have been paralyzed by procrastinations and the foot of fear has kicked us in the ass for years. I for one am sick of it and you should be too. Investing is not only for the wealthy, not only for the other guy. It's for you as well and I will rejoice when you take that first step.

Organic investing, however, extends much further than the stock market for Black America. It must also encompass investing in black businesses and black neighborhoods, and educating our black children.

SAVINGS vs. INVESTING

Black America has been lulled into believing that saving and investing are one in the same. In simple language, saving is when you work for your money and investing is when your money works for you!

When I was in high school, we all attended that one class where you learned how to write a check or open a savings account, but never did I hear one word about investing. The exposure of this concept is still fairly new to the majority of Black America so we continue to march down to the local bank and open a savings account and a checking account and be done with it.

Am I saying you shouldn't save? Absolutely not. I'm saying save better, save smarter and allow your hard earned dollars to reach their maximum potential for growth. Savings and investing are not the same!

BECOMING EMOTIONAL

The one thing I often hear when the market is not fairing so well is, "Rick, I just don't feel right about it." Emotional decisions have sent many people to the poor house. Just think about it. What decision have you ever made based solely on emotion turned out to be a good, sound decision? There is very little room for emotion when building a solid portfolio.

In the 1600s, gift tulips in Holland were given among the wealthy and educated in Europe and Asia, and the demand for tulips went sky high. Some Dutch families went so far as to sell their homes to buy more tulips, hoping for a quick profit. When the bottom fell out of the tulip market, many suffered heavy losses.

This example of emotional investing is not too different from the spike of interest in Internet start-up companies of the late 1990s and early 2000. In retrospect the bubble for overvalued Internet stocks, like the tulips many years ago, was doomed to burst. Asset allocation and proper diversification can insure that you have a better chance at reaching your investment goals. Listed below are some strategies that will help you:

ASSET ALLOCATION

Bear markets only reinforce the importance of time tested investment principles once thought to be out of style or even obsolete. Now is a good time to review your portfolio and determine if the current market has caused your investments to begin missing their objectives.

When considering asset allocation, imagine each asset class inside your portfolio as a car. If your entire portfolio is concentrated in one car, it can easily break down during a market downturn, but if you have a fleet of cars at your disposal in a diversified portfolio, you are better able to withstand market downturns and you can keep on rolling.

DOLLAR COST AVERAGING

With dollar cost averaging, you can buy low or high. When prices are low, you can purchase more shares; shares that can grow when the market recovers. When prices are higher, fewer shares can be purchased. But over time the average amount paid for each share (average cost per share) will usually be less than the average price per share. For example say you are investing two hundred dollars for six months it would look like this:

Month Purch.	Investment	Price Per Share	# of Shares
One	$200	$20	10.00
Two	$200	$15	13.33
Three	$200	$15	13.33
Four	$200	$13	15.38
Five	$200	$10	20.00
Six	$200	$10	20.00

After reviewing the above listed example, you can determine the average cost per share (total investment divided by number of shares bought) $1200 /92.04=13.03. Is less than the Average price per share (the sum of a share price divided by the number of contributions $83/6=$13.83.

Your goal is to have your cost per share to be less than your price for share and the difference, whatever that number is, will be your profit margin.

Many of us putting aside $25, $50 or $100 dollars in a Roth IRA may be dollar cost averaging without even knowing it. If you are working with a financial advisor, discuss your strategies with him or her.

DIVERSIFY! DIVERSIFY! DIVERSIFY!

Asset allocation does not only mean diversifying your money across different asset classes. It also means diversifying within each type of investment in your portfolio. Your investments will fall into one share class or another and based on the economic conditions, you tend to offset losses and spread risk. When building a

143

portfolio, the goal is to keep your mutual fund overlap at ten percent or less. For example:

Portfolio A

Mutual Fund A	Mutual Fund B	Mutual Fund C
Gap	Exxon	Gap
Wal-Mart	Mobil Oil	JC Penny
Nike	BP Oil	Kmart
JC Penny	Getty Oil	Johnson-Johnson
Kmart	Oil Co. A	Oil Co. A
Old Navy	Oil Co. B	Oil Co. B

Analysis: Most mutual funds are made up of ten holdings. I only used six in this example. In Portfolio A, you can see that although there are a number of holdings, the funds are not diversified within each mutual fund nor is the overlap less than ten percent. In Mutual Fund A and Mutual Fund C, three of the six holdings are exactly the same. This means that your risk is increasingly higher and so is your exposure to loss. Further, Mutual Fund A and Mutual Fund B have the same type of companies, therefore in Mutual Fund B, if the oil industry goes down, the entire fund will suffer great losses. Now look at the

Portfolio B below:

Mutual Fund A	Mutual Fund B	Mutual Fund C
Wal-Mart	Berkshire Hathaway	Treasury Notes
Microsoft	Exxon	Gov't Bonds
Johnson-Johnson	JP Morgan Chase	Bond A
Phillip Morris	Pfizer	Bond B
Company A	Lockhead Martin	Bond C
Company B	Wal-mart	Bond D

Analysis: Portfolio B shows a greater degree of diversification thereby offering the best opportunity for wealth accumulation. Because the individual mutual funds are diversified, it allows the entire portfolio to remain at ten percent overlap, thereby maximizing your ability to grow wealth.

OVERLAP

Your goal when building a portfolio is to remain as diversified as possible. The fact that your portfolio has a considerable amount of mutual funds is not proof that your portfolio is diversified. Rule of thumb is that your portfolio should be at ten percent or less.

I encourage you to go and pull out all of your investment portfolio information, whether it is a 401k, 403b, IRA or other. Look at the holdings in your portfolio, recognize the companies in each fund and see which funds have the same companies. In the funds that have, 3, 4, or more of the same companies, considering replacing those funds with funds that will lower your overlap and increase you diversification.

TIMING THE MARKET

There is an old adage in the financial world, "it is not timing, it is **time in** the market". One of your most powerful weapons against short-term volatility is long-term thinking!!!

Because the stock market and other investment vehicles fluctuate, you may be tempted to try and time your investments. That is attempting to move your money into a particular investment vehicle to achieve the maximum performance. While this may seem like the proper thing to do, it very rarely is an effective strategy.

It's almost impossible for even financial experts to predict the Market's highs and lows and secondly, stocks tend to experience the bulk of their gains in single-day performances. When you miss even one day or a handful of the Market's best days can significantly reduce your investment gains.

CONSISTENTCY

One of the best ways to deal with an uncertain market is to stick with your long-term plan. It's kind of like working on a marriage for many years. My mom and dad have been married for over fifty years and they would both tell you that the marriage has been the best investment of their lives. I would be willing to bet you that at one point or another they wanted to pull out of that investment. But they stayed in it, looked at the long-term rewards and continue to invest.

One piece of advice my dad gave me when I was considering marriage was probably one of the simplest and most brilliant things I've ever heard. He said, "Stay Consistent". I would like to pass that piece of advice onto you right now regarding your investment portfolio.

Between 1926 and 2000, stocks posted negative returns in 21 years or about once every three to five years. Of course, this also means that stocks went up in 54 years. If you plan to be invested for any length of time, down years are an inevitable part of experience.

If you are investing $25, $50 or whatever per month, stay your course and you will realize your retirement goals.

LONG-TERM GOALS REQUIRE LONG-TERM THINKING

READING AND UNDERSTANDING STOCK QUOTES

Before I understood how to read and decipher the financial pages of the newspaper, they were quite intimidating and often times that part of the paper was quickly discarded or maybe lining someone's birdcage. Well, knowledge is power. Lets get going!

NAV stands for the "Net Asset Value Per Share" of the offering price including Net Asset Value plus the maximum sales charge, if any. (Remember, mutual funds use forward pricing which means you will always find quotes the day after the Market closes. For example, you will find Tuesday's quotations in Wednesday's paper.)

There is no high, low and close. Unlike the New York Stock Exchange, mutual fund prices are only computed once a day. The quotations begin by listing the mutual fund's name, abbreviated and alphabetically. Whenever you see the name in bold print and then numerous funds under the heading, it indicates a family of funds under the same distributorship.

Column B is the net asset followed by the public offering price. If the fund is a no-load fund, the initials **NL** appear in the offering price column because the offering price and the net asset value (NAV) are the same. When you review funds with a sales load, the difference between the Net Asset Value and the public offering price is the sales load. The last column is the change in net asset value from the preceding day's computation.

You will also be able to determine if the fund has a redemption fee or an annual 12b-1 fee that was mentioned earlier. If the fund name is followed by the letter **R**, the fund has a redemption fee (a back end load). If the fund is followed by the letter **P**, the fund has an annual 12b-1 fee to compensate for commissions, sales literature, distribution cost and other built-in costs. If the fund name is followed by the letter **T**, the fund has both a redemption fee as well as 12b-1 fees.

Now let's read a couple of quotes shall we:

Tuesday, July 26, 1999

	NAV	Offer Price	NAV Chg
Abc Cap:			
Global t	11.97	12.60	-03
International p	5.75	6.05	+02
Gloster Funds			
Bond	8.75	NL	-05
Int'l Stk r	15.15	15.45	+15

Example: You purchased shares of the Gloster Bond fund on July 25th, 1999. What is the price you would have paid per share? Answer, $8.80

Remember, that prices will always be a day behind, therefore the net asset value (NAV) was $8.75 as of the computation on July 26th. That represented a 5 cent change from the previous day. Since you purchased the day before (July 25th) and the fund is a no load fund, you would have purchased the day before for a nickel higher.

Let's go again just to make sure: You are selling 500 shares of ABC Capital Global Fund on Monday, July 25th. How much would your shares be worth? Answer, $6000.

Remember, you sold on the 25th of July and there was a 3-cent change; Tuesday's NAV was $11.97. That means that you would receive 3 cent more and because the fund is followed by a "p", 12b-1 fee will apply.

Understanding this methodology will have you running to the nearest Wall Street Journal. The fear of the unknown melts away and is replaced with a glacier of information. Investing in the stock market will be a less daunting task.

RICK'S PICKS

There are thousands of mutual funds for you to invest your hard earned money. However, there are very few mutual fund companies owned by black Americans. I encourage you to research the companies listed below, contact them, and request a prospectus. In my opinion, these black-owned mutual fund companies are some of the brightest stars in the investment universe.

Ariel Funds
200 East Randolph Drive Ste. 2900
Chicago, Illinois 60601
(800) 292-7435
www.arielmutualfunds.com

Holland Capital
One North Wacker Drive Ste.700
Chicago, Illinois 60606
(800) 522-2711
www.hollandcap.com

Brown Capital Management, Inc.
1201 North Calvert Street
Baltimore, Maryland 21202
(800) 809-fund
www.browncapital.com

The Edgar Lomax Company
6564 Loisdale Court
Springfield, Virginia 22150
(866) 205-0524
www.edgarlomax.com

The Calvert Group
4550 Montgomery Avenue
Bethseda, Maryland 20814
(800) 368-2748
www.calvertgroup.com

     The first black owned company to go public on the New York Stock Exchange was Parks Sausage Company. Since that time, other black owned companies have gone public and made tremendous strides and have paved the way for many companies to come, Those companies are listed below:

Advanced Engineering Design (AED)
American Shared Hospital Services (AMS)
American Stock Exchange
Ault, Inc. (AULT) NASDAQ
Baoa (BAOA) NASDAQ
BET Holdings (BTU) NYSE
Caraco Pharmaceutical Lab (CARA) NASDAQ
Granite Broadcasting (CBTVK) NASDAQ
Myriad Intl (MRAD) NASDAQ
Pyrocap Intl (PYOC) NASDAQ
United American Health Care (UAH) NYSE

I would encourage you to research these companies. Learn all that you can about them and then support them, invest in them and watch them and your money grow.

The ten largest mutual fund companies in the United States as of 2002 are listed below:

1. Fidelity Investments
2. Vanguard
3. Capital Research and Management
4. Merrill Lynch
5. Morgan Stanley & Company
6. Putnam Funds
7. Federated Investors
8. Dreyfus Corporation
9. Franklin Templeton Companies
10. Citi Group Asset Management

These companies are ranked by assets under management, but remember bigger does not equate to better. Invest black dollars in black companies.

CHAPTER NINE

WHY BLACK AMERICA MUST INVEST!!

You must become a great finisher in a world of starters.

When I was growing up in Kansas City, I used to see my dad pull out his wallet and take the rubber bands from around it before he could open it. I asked him why did he have rubber bands around his wallet and his response was, "son, this is my extra security." I shared that with you because thirty years later my dad still uses those rubber bands on his wallet. Now I am not sure he uses the same rubber bands or even if he still thinks he needs them for security, but I think he uses them out of habit and the fact that it feels familiar. It is the insidious weed of familiarity and doubt that has choked the flowers in the garden of black American investors. Now is the time for us to expand our thinking past what is familiar and venture into unfamiliar investment territory. You can be safe and still become a successful investor.

As I mentioned in an earlier chapter, when I received my license to sell securities, I felt an enormous sense of accomplishment and happiness. I truly felt that black Americans would beat a path to my door because I could help, but that never happened.

I once worked for one of the largest insurance companies in the industry that sold any investment you can imagine. I remember sitting in the Director of Sales office one day reviewing my productivity and listening to his disappointment that my numbers were down. When I explained that my client base was mostly black and had not accumulated great amounts of wealth, his response was, "maybe your clients are not consistent with the goals of this firm." I knew right then that I had to do something different and I resigned from that company.

WHAT YOU MUST DO

- Live beneath your means or at least equal to them
- Pay Yourself First
- Create a plan TODAY!
- Stick to the plan
- Understand how your retirement plan works
- Make a Will
- Get rid of debt
- Stay focused
- Understand that investments are long term
- Stop making excuses
- Get started today!

Like many of us, I was recently faced with the challenge of losing a few pounds to stay in shape. I immediately went out and purchased a bicycle and started to ride through my neighborhood. As I rode passed one manicured lawn after another, the one startling denominator were the vehicles in the driveways. What I witnessed was a collection of vehicles that would rival that of any classic car showroom. It is beyond my comprehension why an individual with a monthly mortgage of eight hundred dollars per month would have a car payment of five, six, seven hundred dollars or more. If you own a home worth $100,000, your car should not be worth $50,000. Living equal to or below our means is one of black Americans' biggest hurdles to achieving retirement success.

Black Americans are earning more money than ever before but the wealth accumulation between black Americans and white Americans is wider than ever. As black Americans, we must get in the habit of paying ourselves first!!!

By deducting a small amount of each paycheck, you begin a systematic and disciplined approach to building your retirement nest egg.

<u>CREATE A SPENDING PLAN</u>

Create an amount that you can save without making drastic changes to your spending habits or lifestyle. The amount recommended is ten percent of your take home pay. If you realize that your total is a negative number or less than what you would like to save, you need to re-evaluate your plan and see where you may be able to cut costs.

Keep a written record of all of your expenditures for one month so you will know exactly where your money is going; and yes, include the money you spend at the nightclubs and on adult beverages. Really take a good hard look at where you can cut costs and what you may be able to live without altogether.

Once you have determined what you can save each month, write that figure down and make it one of your permanent expenditures. Before you pay anyone else, pay yourself first with every paycheck you earn. Recognize that emergencies arise, but do not be discouraged. Stay the course and realize your dreams.

NO SOCIAL SECURITY

If you think that social security will be there for you, you may want to think again. The maximum annual Social Security benefit in 2002 was $19,920 and the average, $10,485. These statistics suggest individuals dependent on Social Security will likely face financial difficulties when they retire.

Did you know that by the age of retirement, experts agree that between 70-80% of pre-retirement income will be needed to support a comparable lifestyle. Furthermore, to keep pace with inflation, that dollar amount will have to increase yearly.

A good portion of society believe that because you have paid into Social Security for the majority of your working life, that it will meet you at retirement when you get there. The current system dictates that at age 65, you will receive an average of your 35 highest salary years. You also can collect eighty percent of your benefits at age sixty-two but the retirement age is scheduled to gradually increase. So understand that the current Social Security system may not be the system that you will be a beneficiary of. If you are 40 years old or younger, you will have to work longer and may have a much smaller benefit.

MAKING A WILL

Do you have a will? Don't feel bad. You are in the majority of black Americans. Most black Americans die without ever creating one. Now you may be thinking, "I don't have anything to leave anyone", but I beg to differ. As morbid as it sounds, a will allows you to make your wishes known from the grave. Wills are not just for the rich; the amount of property you have is irrelevant. A will's primary function is to ensure that your assets get to the people that you want them to go to. Without a will, it's possible that all or a portion of your assets will be claimed by the state in which you died.

Short of running down to the local office supply store and purchasing that "making a will kit" you should know that a will consist of the twelve basic elements outlined on the following page:

- Name and place of resident
- A brief description of your assets
- Names of all beneficiaries
- Names of alternate beneficiaries
- Special gifts, such as an auto, residence or jewelry
- Establishment of trust, if applicable
- Cancellation of debts owed to you
- Name of executor
- Name of guardian for minor children, if applicable
- Name of an alternative guardian
- Your signature
- Witnesses' signatures

One of the most important items in the will is naming an executor. This is the person that will oversee the distribution of your will. This person should be someone that you can trust to execute your wishes, such as a spouse, adult child, or sibling.

After organizing the objectives of your will, ask yourself lots of questions so that everything is covered. Take inventory of all of your assets and remember to update your will after any major changes such as new home purchase, inheritances, lottery winnings, etc. Remember to keep your will in a safe place.

I was speaking with a friend of mine and she mentioned to me that her grandmother always paid for everything in cash and she didn't keep her money in the bank. My friend said her grandmother grew up in a time when black

Americans could not trust the bank to be honorable when handling blacks' money. Accounts would have inconsistent balances and in some instances, the money in a bank account would disappear altogether. Those circumstances started generations to distrust and thereby miss out on investment growth. That mentality has been a living breathing albatross around black America's neck for decades.

Friends; I feel that I can call you a friend at this point because we have been through one of the most intimate parts of your life, your finances. I'm confident that this book has accomplished what I said it would. I also have confidence in you, the reader. I cannot tell you how many times I've been thoroughly disappointed when, after speaking with a potential black client, they decide not begin building a retirement portfolio.

The name of this chapter is "Why Black America Must Invest". That question can be answered in so many different ways. As I write this book, one of the oldest, historically black colleges in the United States, is facing a tremendous amount of financial trouble and may very well be on the verge of closing its doors forever.

I could provide you with countless examples of where black Americans placed their retirement destiny in other hands, whether it is the government or a company pension. Or maybe I should ask how many reading this book has a parent, grandparent, aunt or uncle that is at the mercy of public assistance. Black America must invest in order to sustain, maintain and catapult black America into the next generation.

At the end of the day all we have are family, a few good friends, and the grace of God. I pray that you will move forward with your investment plan with a zeal like never before. I pray that you get out of those lines purchasing lottery tickets and stand in a line with a financial advisor at the end of it.

The great African-American author, Ralph Ellison, wrote, "I am an invisible man. No I am not a spook like those who haunted Edgar Allan Poe. Nor am I one of your Hollywood-movie ectoplasms. I am a man of substance, of flesh and bone, fiber and liquids and I might even be said to possess a mind. I am invisible understand, simply because people refuse to see me."

I challenge you to not remain invisible in the world of investments. I pray good health for you and your family and as I said in the very beginning, we are in this together. If you have any questions that you cannot get answered write me and I will get them answered for you. So at the end of the day, you ask yourself, "am I black or am I black and green?"

THE LINGO

Many terms have been discussed in this book. Hopefully this glossary will be one you can use for many years.

Accumulation Unit - The unit used to measure the value of the separate account of an annuity during the pay in phase. Usually valued on a daily basis, and will fluctuate in value based on the performance of the investments chosen.

Annuitize - The time in which an annuity holder elects to begin the pay out of his annuity product. This payout follows the accumulation phase, usually at retirement age.

Annuity - An investment vehicle in which an investor contributes money into a plan and receives payout in a fixed or variable amount. This vehicle has tax deferred growth of earnings during the accumulation phase, but you will be taxed at ordinary income rates on everything exceeding the cost basis.

Annuity Unit - Unit used to value the separate account of an annuity during the payout phase. The number of annuity units is a fixed amount designated when electing to annuitize.

Ask Price - The price of a mutual fund at which the mutual fund shares can be purchased.

Asset Allocation - The shared amount of the investment portfolio among categories of assets, such as money market accounts, stocks, bonds and even tangible assets such as precious metals or real estate.

Assets - Everything of value that you own that will create your estate

Assumed Interest Rate (AIR) - A rate stated in a variable annuity that is an assumption of what the separate account will earn during the payout period. Only the first check in the payout period will be calculated on the AIR: all additional payments will fluctuate.

Automatic Reinvestment-The choice made available to mutual fund holders whereby the funds income dividends and capital gains distributions are automatically put back into the fund to buy new shares and thereby build additional holdings.

Bear Market - A declining securities market in terms of price.

Bearish Approach - A strategy an investor takes when he or she thinks that securities prices will decline.

Bid - The highest price anyone has declared that he will pay for a security at a given time.

Blue Chip - A common stock of a large corporation with a stable record of earnings and dividend payments over many years. *(ex. Coca Cola or IBM.)*

Bond - A certificate representing creditorship to raise long-term funds, this product is as though you loaned a business or government entity money.

Break Point - The dollar level in which an investment qualifies for a discounted sales share on a quantity purchase of shares

Bull Market - A rising securities market in terms of price.

Bullish Approach - The strategy an investor takes when he or she thinks security prices will rise.

Capital Gain - The profit from the sale of a capital asset. They can be short term (12 months or less) or long term (more than 12 months)

Capital Loss - A method used to offset the capital gains to establish a net position for tax purposes

Certificate of Deposit (CD) - An interest bearing security, usually issued by commercial banks against money deposited for a specified period of time. Certificates of deposit vary in size and are sometimes called **Jumbo CDs.** These are usually $100,000 and are unsecured by a specific bank.

Common Stock - Pure ownership in a company, common stock holders are junior to all others in the event of a liquidation such as preferred stocks or bonds. However owners of this kind of stock exercise greater control and have a greater opportunity to benefit from dividends and capital appreciation.

Common Stock Fund - A mutual fund that consists mainly of common stocks. The goal of this fund is usually growth.

Convertibles - Bonds and preferred stock that have a convertible feature which gives the holder the right to exchange his security for common stock for a certain period on a fixed or sliding scale of exchange.

Current Yield - When referring to stocks, it is the annual dividend divided by the current ask price. When referring to bonds, it is the annual interest divided by the current market value. *Simply put, what you get divided by what you pay.*

Death Benefit Provision - The provision of an annuity which allows the payment to a beneficiary the greater of the value of the contributions or the value of, the separate account at the owners death. This provision is usually only effective during the accumulation period of an annuity.

Debenture - An unsecured long- term debt offering by a corporation. The corporation only promises its general assets as protection for its creditors.

Deferred Annuity - This annuity will allow the annuitant to accrue earnings in the separate account, tax-deferred, during the accumulation phase.

Discount Bond - Any bond that sells at a price below its face amount on the open market usually when interest rates have risen since the bonds initial issuance.

Discretionary Account - An account whereby the customer authorizes in writing a registered representative to use his or her own judgment in buying and selling securities on behalf of the customer. (I do not suggest this type of account unless you have a very good relationship with the registered representative.)

Diversification - Investing in a number of different security issues for the purpose of reducing and spreading risks.

Dividends - Distributions to stockholders earned and declared by the corporate board of directors.

Dollar Cost Averaging - Whereby an investor invest equal amounts of money in equal intervals no matter if the stock market is moving up or down. This will reduce the average share cost by automatically acquiring more shares in periods of low security prices and fewer shares in periods of high prices.

Equity - The ownership interest of stocks, both common and preferred in a company. This term also refers to excess of value of securities over the debit balance in a general account.

Estate Tax - A tax imposed by a state or the federal government on all assets a person possesses at the time of death.

Face Value - The value of a bond or preferred stock at the time of redemption. Also referred to as **par value**.

Fiduciary - A person with legal rights and powers to act for the benefit of another person.

Fixed Annuity - An insurance product that provides a lifetime retirement income in sum certain (fixed) installments. Both investment and mortality risk are assumed by the insurance company that issues the policy.

General Account - The account into which premium revenues received by the insurance company are deposited. These funds are invested in safe instruments.

Hedge Fund - A mutual fund company which hedges its market commitment by holding securities it believes are likely to increase in value. The sole objective of this type of fund is capital appreciation and it is highly aggressive.

Individual Retirement Account - A personal, tax-deferred retirement account that an employed person may initiate with a deposit limited to $3000 per year. The new tax law (Egtrra) will allow for additional contributions annually up to the year 2005.

Investment Income - Invest income is divided into two types; gross and net;
Gross Investment Income - The total amount of dividends received from an investment company's investments prior to any deductions or expenses.
Net Investment Income - Balance of gross income after payment of all operating expenses. If at least 90% is distributed to shareholders, tax is only paid on undistributed income.

Legal Investment - A security that meets the specifications of various states.

Life Annuity - This is a settlement option chosen by an annuitant that provides retirement income for the lifespan of the annuitant. There are no guarantees other than the life of the annuitant

Liquidity - The ability to easily convert securities holding to cash by an investor and also the ability of the market to absorb a reasonable amount of trading at a reasonable price. Liquidity is considered one of the most important characteristics of a good market.

Load - Also called a sales charge it is the part of the offering price of shares in a mutual fund that covers sales commissions and additional cost of distribution.

Mutual Fund - A financial institution whose business is investing others money. By pooling their resources, investors obtain professional supervision and diversification of their investments.

National Association of Securities Dealers Automated Quotations (NASDAQ) - An electronic data terminal device furnishing its subscribers with instant identification of market makers and their current quotations, updated continuously.

Net Asset Value - The market worth of a mutual fund's total resources, after deduction of liabilities, divided by the number of shares outstanding. It is usually the price at which a share is redeemed.

No-Load Mutual Funds - Mutual funds offered directly to the public at net asset value, with no sales charge. These funds do not offer any professional management.

Nominal Yield - The annual interest rate payable on a bond. It is specified in the indenture and printed on the face of the certificate. Also known as a coupon rate.

Offer - The price at which a person is ready to sell.

Option - A vehicle that conveys to the holder, for a stated period, the holder has certain rights with regard to the underlying security of that option. There are two types of options, call and put. A call option gives the owner the right to buy. A put option is the right to sell.

Par - This is an arbitrary dollar amount assigned to a share of common stock by the corporation's charter.

Point - When referring to stocks, a point indicates one dollar. Since a bond is quoted as a percentage of $1000, a point indicates ten dollars.

Portfolio - Holdings of securities by an individual or institution.

Preferred Stock - This stock allows its owner the entitlement of a fixed dividend to be paid regularly before dividends are paid to common stock holders.

Prospectus - A document stating material information for an impending offering of securities that is used for solicitation purposes.

Real Estate Investment Trust (reit) - An organization that invest in real properties or mortgages and distributes a percentage of its earnings to investors. In most reits, shares may be bought on the open market after the public offering is over.

Redemption Price - The amount per share the mutual fund shareholder receives when he or she cashes in their shares. Also known as a bid price.

Risk - Uncertainty in the market. There are six categories of risk: Market, Financial, Credit, Liquidity, Money rate, Inflation.

Securities - Any note including stocks, bonds, profit sharing agreements, interest in oil and gas rights, variable annuities.

Securities Investor Protection Corporation (sipc) - A government-sponsored and private corporation that guarantees repayment of any money and securities in customer accounts valued at up to five hundred thousand dollars per separate customer ($100,000 cash) in the event of a broker/dealer bankruptcy.

Series EE Savings Bonds - non-marketable federal savings bonds of various denominations offered at a price below face value and redeemed at face value at a later time.

Series HH Savings Bonds - Non marketable federal savings bonds of various denominations offered and redeemed at face value, bearing interest every six months during its lifetime.

Spread - The difference in value between the bid and the offering prices or the difference between the public offering price and the amount received by the issuer

Stock - Certificates representing ownership in a corporation. These certificates may yield dividends and may appreciate or decline in value

Treasury Bill - A certificate that entitles the holder a federal obligation in denominations of $1000 to one million dollars, usually with a maturity date of three to six months. It trades at a discount from face value

Treasury Bond - A federal obligation with maturity rates up to thirty years, with a fixed interest rate. Treasury bonds are traded as a percentage of their face value.

Treasury Note - A federal obligation with maturity rates up to ten years with a fixed rate of interest These notes are traded as a percentage of there face value.

Treasury Stock - These are shares of stock that have been reacquired by its corporation through purchase or donation they are not used for dividends or voting.

Uniform Gift/Transfer To Minors Act (ugma/utma) - A procedure followed when making a gift of securities or cash to a minor. A custodian is appointed by the donor and the securities are registered in the name of the custodian. Only one custodian per minor can be named and the custodian must be an adult. The account has the social security number and tax liability of the minor. If the child is under 14 years of age and has more than $1,400 dollars in unearned income, the excess over $1,400 dollars is taxed to the child but at his or her parents' highest rate.

Yield - Also known as the rate of return it is the dividends or interest paid by a company on its security holdings expressed as a percentage of the current price.

Zero Coupon Bond - A debt security without a stated interest rate. All zero coupon bonds are issued and traded at a discount from their par value.

SOURCES

African-American Desk Reference
Oppenheimer Funds
One Group Funds
U.S. Census Bureau
The Wall Street Journal
The Ariel Report
The Atlanta Journal Constitution
Smart Money Magazine Article
Bisys Education Services
Saving for College.com
Personal Experience

<u>NOTES</u>

ABOUT THE AUTHOR

Rick Knight is a native of Kansas City, Missouri. His areas of expertise include working with small business retirement plans, retirement plans for non-profit organizations, and risk management. Additionally, Rick works with families to develop strategies for retirement, college fund design, and estate planning.

Rick holds six professional securities and insurance licenses, and has worked in the financial services industry for over seven years. He completed his undergraduate studies while proudly serving in the United States Army and earned a Bachelors degree in Political Science.

Rick, has been a recurring guest speaker on WIBB 97.9 fm in Macon, Georgia and has also been a guest speaker of the Charles Ross radio program.

Rick is a member of the Board of Directors for the Boys and Girls Club of Crawford County. He currently resides in Jonesboro, Georgia.